Goodness Gracious

Recipes for Good Food and Gracious Living

Recipes by Roxie Kelley

Illustrations by
Shelly Reeves Smith

Andrews McMeel
Publishing

Kansas City

04 05 06 WKT 10 9 8 7 6 5 4 3

Library of Congress Cataloging-in-Publication Data
Kelley, Roxie.
   Goodness gracious : recipes for good food and gracious living / recipes by Roxie Kelley and friends ; illustrated by Shelly Reeves Smith.
      p. cm.
   ISBN 0-7407-2720-6
1. Cookery, American. I. Title.
   TX715 .K292 2002
   641.5973–dc21   2002074794

ATTENTION: SCHOOLS AND BUSINESSES

Andrews McMeel books are available at quantity discounts with bulk   purchase for educational, business, or sales promotional use. For information, please write to: Special Sales Department, Andrews McMeel Publishing, 4520 Main Street, Kansas City, Missouri 64111.

Presented To:

For You

To my mom,
Mary Phyllis
A picture of a woman
Ever growing
in grace.
With love from Roxie
—RK

To
Mother Hen
with love
—SRS

© 2002 SRS

Table of Contents

Appetizers

Soups & Salads

Main Dishes

Side Dishes

Desserts

As I write this note to you, I am sitting amid stacks and stacks of cardboard boxes ~ moving day is only weeks away. Blake and Brooke and I have sold the place we've called "home" for the past eight years of our lives and are looking forward to what's ahead.

Of course, we're looking back as well. It's hard not to. We have loved this neighborhood and the wonderful people who live here. We love the trees and wildlife and the view out the back door. I'm sure we'll miss it in more ways than we can understand at this point in time. It occurred to me today that this is another phase in my life where it will be important to meet the unpredictable with a certain measure of grace.

That brings us to the subject of this book. Those of you who have purchased other books created by Shelly and me know that we can't just put together a simple cookbook

(continued on the next page...)

Royal Garden

filled with one recipe after another.
It seems we are always driven to bring you
something more. And so, this book is not just
about good food, but also about gracious living.
　　　　This term will no doubt mean different things
　　to different people. Hopefully, before you turn
　　the last page, you will know not only what it
means to me but learn what it means to you.

　　The recipes within these pages come from hours and
hours of experimentation in dozens of different
kitchens. Some are favorites of mine and some of the
recipes come from the kitchens of treasured friends
and family members. All the people who share these
time-honored recipes (including me!) want you to
know that: 1) None of us are gourmet cooks, and
2) we are not ashamed to use convenience foods from
time to time. If there is a common thread among
us, it is that the focus in our kitchens is not simply
on food, but on the fun in sharing

　　I'm confident you　will enjoy the beauty, once
again, of Shelly's　　artwork. Thank you so
much for embracing　our work through the
years. I'm hoping　　this book will create a
backdrop for many
wonderful moments
with those you
hold most
Dear.

~ Roxie
　Kelley

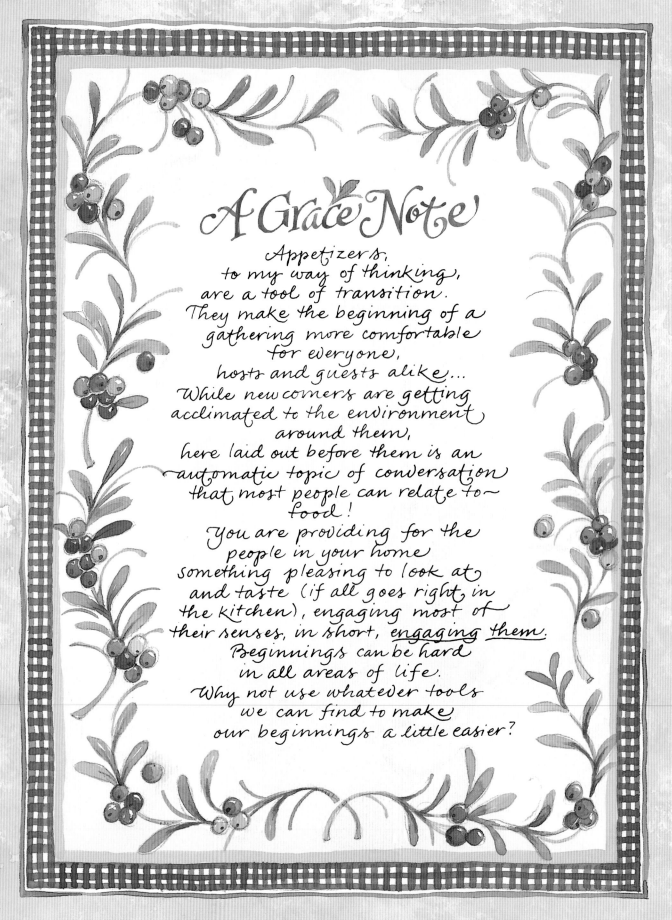

A Grace Note

Appetizers,
to my way of thinking,
are a tool of transition.
They make the beginning of a
gathering more comfortable
for everyone,
hosts and guests alike...
While newcomers are getting
acclimated to the environment
around them,
here laid out before them is an
automatic topic of conversation
that most people can relate to—
food!
You are providing for the
people in your home
something pleasing to look at
and taste (if all goes right in
the kitchen), engaging most of
their senses, in short, engaging them.
Beginnings can be hard
in all areas of life.
Why not use whatever tools
we can find to make
our beginnings a little easier?

Pickle Treats

If there is a party at their dad's house, Blake and Brooke always hope there will be Pickle Treats there. Lori (their sweet step-mom) tells me this recipe comes from Maurice McNabb~ another wonderful teacher / friend from our community. Thank you both.

Softened cream cheese
Thinly sliced cooked ham
Whole sweet pickles

Spread the softened cream cheese over the surface of a slice of ham. Roll the ham and cream cheese around a sweet pickle. Slice into ¼-inch thick rolls and secure with a toothpick from one side or the other.

Arrange the "circles" on a pretty platter and serve.

3

Buffalo Shrimp

½ cup flour
1 teaspoon salt
¼ teaspoon paprika
¼ teaspoon cayenne pepper
12 large uncooked shrimp
¼ cup hot sauce
¼ cup fat-free buttery spread
1 tablespoon water

Preheat the oven to 450 degrees. Line a cookie sheet with a piece of aluminum foil. In a small bowl, make the breading by combining the flour, salt, paprika, and cayenne pepper.

Prepare the shrimp by cutting off the entire shell except the last segment and the tail fins. Remove the vein from the back and clean the shrimp. Then cut a deeper slice where you removed the vein so you can "butterfly" the shrimp (spread the meat out).

Spray the foil on the baking sheet with nonstick olive oil spray. Roll each of the shrimp in the flour mixture. Then arrange them on the baking sheet with the tails sticking up. Spray each shrimp with a coating of nonstick spray. Bake for 10-12 minutes or until golden brown. Then turn the oven to broil for 4-5 minutes. Broil until the shrimp begin to brown and become crispy.

While the shrimp cooks, prepare the sauce by combining the hot sauce with the fat-free butter-flavored spread and a tablespoon of water in a small saucepan. Cook over medium heat until it starts to bubble, stirring occasionally. Then reduce the heat to low and cover until the shrimp are ready. When shrimp are done, remove from the oven, and let rest for 1 minute. Put shrimp into a plastic container with a lid and cover with the sauce. Cover and shake the shrimp until each one is well coated with sauce. Pour the shrimp out onto a plate and serve hot.

Serves 2.

Baked Brie

Served with fresh fruit, there is nothing more elegant or satisfying as an appetizer.

1 (1-pound) package phyllo dough

½ cup butter, melted

1½ pounds Brie, cut into 8 wedges

An assortment of grapes, strawberries, apple wedges

Unroll the phyllo sheets and keep them covered with plastic wrap to prevent them from drying out. Remove two sheets and brush the top one with the butter. Place a wedge of the Brie diagonally on the phyllo sheet, about 2 inches from one corner. Fold the phyllo to cover the cheese and continue to roll the cheese up in the sheet. Fold the ends in when half the phyllo is used up. Roll until the whole sheet is used and the Brie is neatly packaged. Brush the outside with butter to prevent flaking. Repeat with other wedges of Brie and the rest of the phyllo sheets. Chill the wrapped Brie for 30 minutes.

Preheat the oven to 400 degrees. Bake for 10-12 minutes (or until golden brown) on an ungreased cookie sheet. Line a basket with a napkin and gently place the baked Brie in it. Arrange the fruit around it and serve.

Makes 6~8 servings.

Sheila's Shrimp Dip

Sheila Eubank has been a special friend to both Shelly and me. We feel blessed that our paths crossed with that of this very talented and thoughtful lady. Time spent with Sheila is comforting and inspirational. What more could you ask for in a friend!

4 (8-ounce) packages cream cheese
1 small yellow onion, peeled and diced
1 large tomato, peeled and diced
4 medium hot banana pepper slices, seeded and diced.
2 hot chile pepper slices, diced (optional, for those who like _hot_)
3/4 pound steamed and peeled shrimp, chopped
Garlic salt to taste

Melt the cream cheese in a Crock-Pot and add the other ingredients. Serve the dip warm with tortilla chips. Serves about 20.

Note: You may substitute 1 cup of salsa for the onion and tomato, but add slowly so the dip doesn't get too thin.

7

Quesadillas

These simple quesadillas are great as an appetizer. To expand on this recipe, you can add diced grilled shrimp, chicken, or beef and turn it into a main dish.

½ cup diced red onion
½ sweet red bell pepper, seeded and diced
1 clove garlic, minced
2 tablespoons olive oil
½ teaspoon salt
12 (8-inch) flour tortillas
2 cups grated cheese, either Cheddar or Monterey Jack, or a combination of both.

Sauté onion, red pepper and garlic in 1 tablespoon of the oil until tender, about 5-7 minutes. Season with salt. Spread ⅓ cup of this mixture on each of 6 tortillas. Sprinkle with grated cheese and top with another tortilla. Lightly oil skillet and brown each quesadilla on both sides until golden. Cut into wedges and serve with salsa.

Serves about 10-12 as an appetizer, or 4-6 as a main dish.

Caramel Apple Dip

There is no better snack on a crisp fall day. It can be stored in the refrigerator for several weeks in an airtight container.

1 (14-ounce) bag caramels
1 (8-ounce) package cream cheese, softened
½ cup brown sugar
2 tablespoons granulated sugar
1 teaspoon vanilla
¾ cup chopped dry roasted nuts
About 5 apples, cored and sliced

Gradually melt the caramels in microwave, stirring every 30 seconds until soft. Be careful not to scorch! Stir in the cream cheese, sugars, vanilla, and nuts. Dip the apple slices into the caramel mixture. This serves as a yummy ice cream topping as well. Yields 8-10 servings.

© 2001 SRS

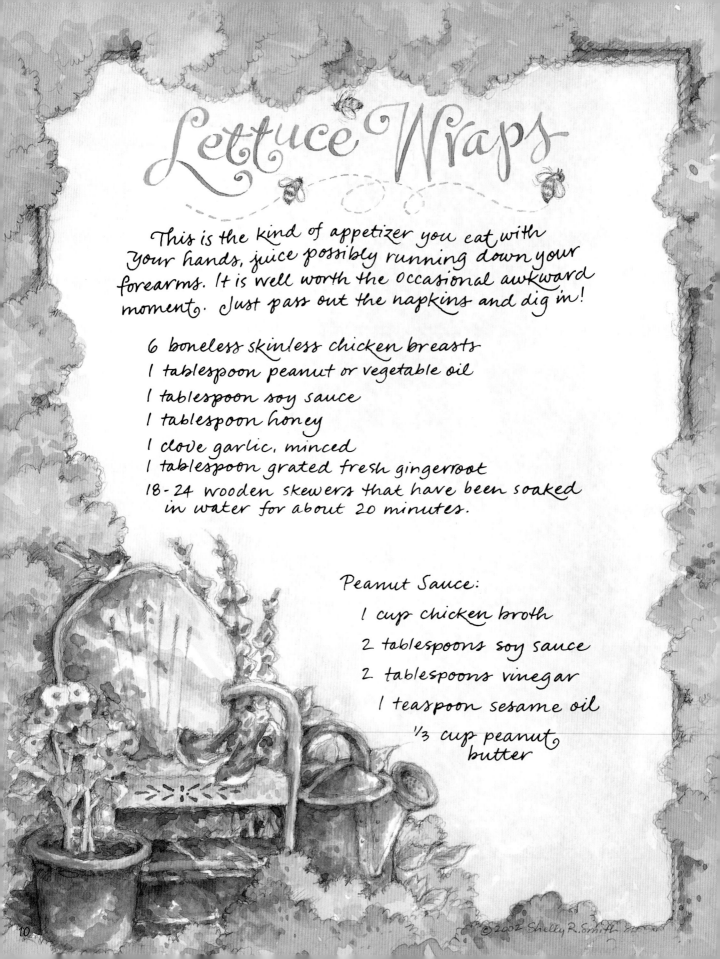

Lettuce Wraps

This is the kind of appetizer you eat with your hands, juice possibly running down your forearms. It is well worth the occasional awkward moment. Just pass out the napkins and dig in!

6 boneless skinless chicken breasts
1 tablespoon peanut or vegetable oil
1 tablespoon soy sauce
1 tablespoon honey
1 clove garlic, minced
1 tablespoon grated fresh gingerroot
18-24 wooden skewers that have been soaked in water for about 20 minutes.

Peanut Sauce:

1 cup chicken broth

2 tablespoons soy sauce

2 tablespoons vinegar

1 teaspoon sesame oil

1/3 cup peanut butter

© 2002 Shelly R. Smith

Garnish:

Boston Bibb lettuce leaves

2 cups julienned carrots

2 cups peeled, seeded, and
diced cucumbers

1 cup peanuts

Cut the chicken into strips.
Mix the peanut oil, 1 tablespoon
soy sauce, honey, garlic, and ginger in a
medium bowl. Add the chicken and mix until
coated.

Prepare the grill. Thread the chicken onto
skewers and place on hot grill. Discard the
marinade. Grill for about 10 minutes, or until
juices run clear. Turn frequently.

Bring the broth, 2 tablespoons soy sauce,
vinegar, and sesame oil to a simmer in a small
saucepan. Add the peanut butter and stir
until well-blended. Arrange the grilled chicken
on skewers on a platter lined with Boston Bibb
lettuce leaves, julienned carrots, diced
cucumbers, and peanuts. Serve with the
hot peanut sauce for dipping.

Makes 18-24 skewers.

Cheese & Artichoke Torte

This is a beautiful layered appetizer that can be made the night before. I have a giant red platter I like to use when serving this dish.

1 medium sweet red bell pepper
Paper bag
1 jar (6 ounces) marinated artichoke hearts, drained and chopped
2 tablespoons minced fresh parsley
2 (8-ounce) packages cream cheese, softened
1 (1-ounce) package ranch-style dressing mix

Preheat the broiler. Place the whole pepper directly on the oven rack. Broil until sides start to blister and brown. Remove the pepper from the oven and place it in a paper bag. Close and let stand for 20 minutes. Remove the pepper from bag. Peel, seed and chop. Combine the chopped pepper, artichokes and parsley and set aside. In a medium bowl, beat the cream cheese and ranch mix until smooth. Line a 3-cup bowl or dish with plastic wrap. Divide the cheese mixture into thirds and the vegetable mixture in half. Alternate layers of the cheese and vegetable mixtures, beginning and ending with the cheese. Chill at least 4 hours. Invert on a platter. Remove the plastic wrap and serve with assorted crackers.

Serves about 10-12

Mild Sweet Salsa

Some would say this salsa is for wimps. Well, wimps have to eat, too. So put your "we-like-it-hot" prejudices aside and enjoy.

2 large tomatoes, peeled, seeded, and coarsely chopped

½ green pepper, finely chopped

½ sweet red bell pepper, seeded and finely chopped

½ red onion, finely chopped

1 clove garlic, minced

2 tablespoons olive oil

2 tablespoons fresh lime juice

1 tablespoon white wine vinegar

1 tablespoon chopped fresh basil, or ½ teaspoon dried basil

¼ teaspoon dried oregano

½ cup tomato sauce

1 tablespoon sugar

½ cup frozen corn

salt, and pepper to taste

Combine all ingredients and chill, covered, for at least 2 hours.

Makes about 5 cups.

Chicken Fingers with Honey Mustard

This is a sure thing with little ones around your table. In addition to the Honey Mustard, be sure to have plenty of catsup and barbecue sauce on hand, too. The Honey Mustard is best when prepared a day or two in advance.

Honey Mustard:
  ½ cup honey
  ¼ cup Dijon mustard

1 cup flour
½ teaspoon salt
¼ teaspoon pepper
4 boneless, skinless chicken breasts cut into 2-inch strips (or a family-size package of frozen boneless, skinless chicken strips, thawed in the refrigerator)
¾ cup milk
1 cup vegetable oil for frying

To prepare the Honey Mustard, blend the ingredients together in a small bowl and set aside in the refrigerator.

In a shallow bowl, mix the flour, salt and pepper. Dip the chicken in the milk. Roll in the flour mixture to coat well. Place the chicken on waxed paper.

Pour 1/4 inch of the oil into a large skillet. Heat over medium-high heat to about 350 degrees or until a cube of white bread dropped in oil browns evenly in 1 minute. Place the chicken in an even layer in hot oil. Do not crowd. It is better to fry chicken in batches rather than all at one time.

Fry, turning once, for about 3 minutes on each side or until golden brown and crisp.

Drain on paper towels. Pass the sauce.

Serves about 6.

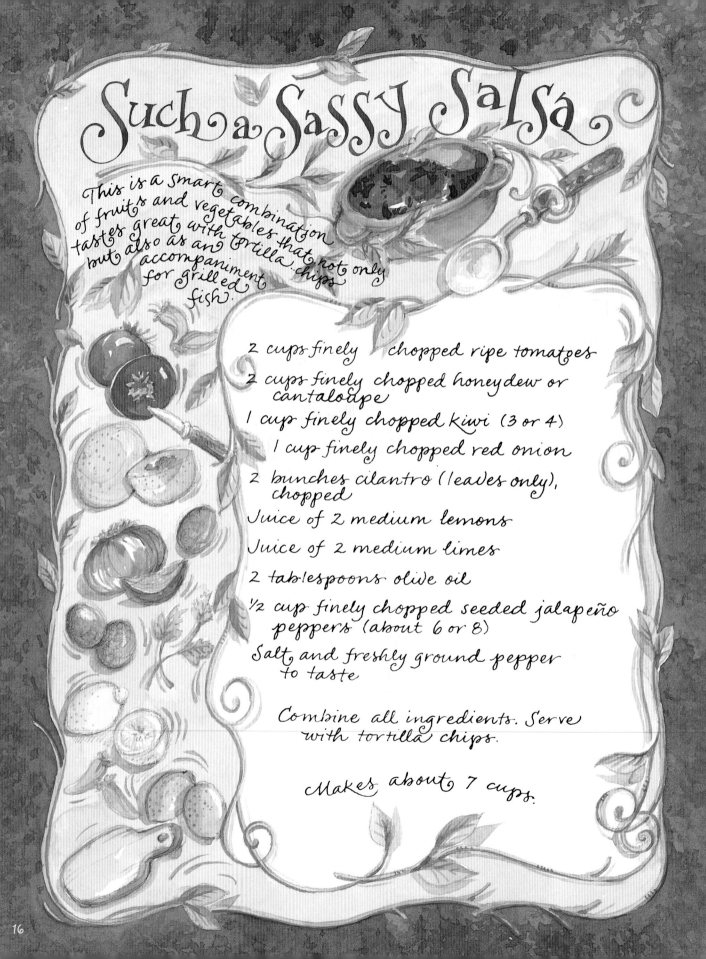

Such a Sassy Salsa

This is a smart combination of fruits and vegetables that not only tastes great with tortilla chips but also as an accompaniment for grilled fish.

2 cups finely chopped ripe tomatoes

2 cups finely chopped honeydew or cantaloupe

1 cup finely chopped kiwi (3 or 4)

1 cup finely chopped red onion

2 bunches cilantro (leaves only), chopped

Juice of 2 medium lemons

Juice of 2 medium limes

2 tablespoons olive oil

½ cup finely chopped seeded jalapeño peppers (about 6 or 8)

Salt and freshly ground pepper to taste

Combine all ingredients. Serve with tortilla chips.

Makes about 7 cups.

Sweet Stuff

To all my fans,

Jana Agniel

This recipe is from Jana Agniel, otherwise known as "The Katie Couric of Camden County." Jana not only looks like famous Katie, she seems to have many of the same mannerisms. She is pleasant, positive, and energetic, not to mention darn cute.

1 (13.5 ounces) box Rice Chex cereal

1 cup broken nuts (pecans, walnuts, almonds, or cashews will work nicely)

3/4 cup butter

1 2/3 cups brown sugar

1/3 cup granulated sugar

1/4 teaspoon baking soda

In a large microwave-safe bowl, mix the cereal and nuts together. Melt the butter in a small saucepan, adding sugars and mixing well. Bring to a boil and add the baking soda. Pour the butter mixture over the cereal mixture. Microwave for 5 minutes, stirring well after each minute. Spread out on waxed paper and cool. Store in an airtight container.

Serves 8-10.

Joyce's
Bacon-Tomato Tartlets

One of the bonuses of being in "retail" is that you get to become friends with your customers. Joyce and Herb Millard have been so generous with their support, enthusiasm, and friendship. I'm happy to be able to share one of Joyce's tasty dishes with you!

1 (17.3-ounce) can flaky biscuits
6 slices bacon, cooked, drained and crumbled
1 medium tomato, seeded and chopped
3 ounces mozzarella cheese, grated
½ onion, chopped
½ cup mayonnaise
1 tablespoon fresh basil leaves, chopped
1 clove garlic, minced
1 teaspoon dried thyme
½ teaspoon dried oregano

Preheat the oven to 350 degrees. Separate each biscuit into three pieces. Spray the mini-muffin tins lightly with cooking oil. Press the split biscuits into the tins. Mix the remaining ingredients together and fill each of the pastries with the mixture. Bake for 10-12 minutes or until golden brown. Can be frozen and reheated for unexpected guests.

Serves 6-8.

Caesar Dip

This is great as a vegetable dip and also as a dressing for sandwiches and salads. It is best prepared the night before serving.

½ cup freshly grated Parmesan cheese

3 canned anchovy fillets, drained

2 tablespoons fresh lemon juice

½ cup fresh parsley chopped

1 tablespoon capers

cracked pepper to taste

1 cup sour cream

Romaine lettuce, inner leaves (rinsed in cold water and thoroughly dried)

In a blender or a food processor, combine the grated Parmesan cheese, anchovy fillets, lemon juice, parsley, capers and cracked pepper. Puree until smooth. Add 3-4 tablespoons sour cream, if necessary to help the mixture puree well. In a small bowl mix puree with the remaining sour cream until well-blended. Cover and chill overnight. The Romaine lettuce will be used for both garnish and dipping.

A Grace Note

I remember a course in high school called "Family Living". It was a semester-long session required of both male and female students and it was supposed to prepare us for real life in a home of our own. We learned about ironing, cooking, cleaning, personal grooming, and even decorating. But the subject of divorce or "blended families" never, ever came up. Actually, I don't think the term "blended family" existed back then, and divorce was not something we discussed very comfortably in or out of school. But, these issues have certainly become reality for so many in our culture.

I think if I had to name one area of my life that provided the greatest lessons in living graciously it would be the day-to-day world of our blended family. Potentially, there is no experience more anxiety-ridden, more humbling than divorce. We seem to be faced with a situation that appears all but broken beyond repair. Those of us who have gone through divorce (or marriage to a divorced person) know intimately these feelings of failure, hurt, disappointment, and fear. If there are children involved, the shame and frustration of not being able to give them something "whole" to build a life on is sometimes overwhelming.

I don't claim to have the "recipe" for a healthy blended family. I only know that in my situation I am blessed with two very loving and gracious people, Kim and Lori Kelley, who are determined to keep forgiveness, supportiveness and positive communication at the top of their list of priorities where our families are concerned. I thank God that through His grace my children have a wonderful father and step-mom to love and support them each minute they are away from me.

If someone were to ask me what purpose I wish this book could serve, I hope you would allow me this one lofty dream ~ that way beyond the pleasure of food and the subject of hospitality ~ that families everywhere could learn to live above their past failures, judgements, and disappointments with a grace and love that surpasses all understanding.

Breads & Muffins

© 2001 Shelly Reeves Smith

Pam's Rolls

I can't think of Pam Chiles without breathing a prayer of thanks for what her friendship means to my sister, Jan. She is a priceless person and a wonderful cook.

1 (¼-ounce) package yeast

1 cup lukewarm water

½ cup sugar

3 eggs, beaten

3/4 cup unsalted butter, melted

¼ teaspoon salt

4 cups flour

Dissolve the yeast in lukewarm water. Add the sugar, eggs, and butter. Add the salt to the flour and blend into the liquid with mixer. Place the dough in a buttered bowl and cover loosely with plastic wrap

©2002 SRS

sprayed with vegetable oil spray. Place in refrigerator overnight.

The next day, divide the dough into three pieces. Roll out each piece out on a floured surface into a circle a little thicker than pie crust. Cut the circle into twelve triangles. Roll each triangle from wide end to small end. Repeat with the rest of the dough. Place on baker's paper a few inches apart and form into crescents. Cover loosely with plastic wrap. Let rise at room temperature until doubled in size.

Preheat oven to 350 degrees. Bake until light golden brown (about 10-15 minutes). Makes 2 dozen rolls.

Grandma Pat's Banana Bread

Pat O'Rourke was in my store one fall day and we visited about a cookbook she was compiling. She was kind enough to share this recipe with me. I hope you enjoy it as much as I do.

3/4 cup bananas, mashed
1/2 cup margarine
1 cup sugar
2 eggs, beaten slightly
1 1/4 cups flour
1 teaspoon baking soda
1 teaspoon salt
1/2 cup broken pecans

Preheat the oven to 325 degrees. Cream together the bananas, margarine and sugar. Add the eggs and mix. Then add the rest of the ingredients and mix well. Pour into a 9 x 5 x 3-inch greased loaf pan. Bake 45-55 minutes until golden brown or until a toothpick inserted in the center comes out clean.

Serves 8-10.

Country-Style Cheese Biscuits

These biscuits are wonderful with breakfast or brunch, or even with a hearty stew for your evening meal.

4 cups flour

2 tablespoons baking powder

4 teaspoons sugar

½ teaspoon salt

½ cup shredded Cheddar cheese

¼ cup thinly sliced green onion

2 cups half-and-half

½ cup butter, melted

Preheat the oven to 375 degrees. In a large bowl, stir the dry ingredients together. Add the cheese and the green onion, and then add the half-and-half. Mix gently to form a soft, moist dough. Turn the dough out onto a lightly floured surface and knead for 2 minutes. Do not overknead. Pat the dough out to a thickness of 1 inch. Using a 2-inch biscuit cutter or a glass, cut out the biscuits. Dip each into the melted butter to coat lightly on both sides. Arrange the biscuits on a baking sheet and bake for 15-18 minutes or until golden. Makes 18.

Apple Streusel

TEA LOAF

One of my fall favorites!

2 cups flour

1 tablespoon baking powder

½ teaspoon salt

½ cup sugar plus 2 tablespoons

½ cup butter

2 cups chopped peeled apples

½ teaspoon lemon zest

½ cup milk

1 egg

½ teaspoon ground cinnamon

Preheat the oven to 350 degrees. In a large bowl, stir together the flour, baking powder, salt, and ½ cup sugar. Cut in the butter until coarse crumbs form. Reserve ½ cup of this mixture. Stir the apples and lemon zest into the remaining flour~butter mixture.

In a small bowl, mix the milk and egg until well~blended. Add to the apple mixture and stir just until moistened. Pour batter into a greased 9 x 5 x 3 - inch loaf pan. In a small bowl, stir the reserved flour~butter mixture, cinnamon, and the remaining 2 tablespoons sugar together. Sprinkle over batter. Press down lightly. Bake 55-60 minutes or until a toothpick inserted in the center comes out clean. Cool in pan 10 minutes before slicing and serving.

Makes 1 loaf.

Focaccia

This recipe for Italian flat bread is so versatile. Choose from any of the recommended toppings below to suit your family's taste.

1 (¼ ounce) package dry yeast
¾ cup warm water
2 cups flour
½ teaspoon salt
4 tablespoons olive oil

Some Suggested Toppings:

Sliced black olives, shaved prosciutto,
chopped leeks, rosemary,
freshly ground pepper and/or kosher salt,
thinly sliced red onions, thinly sliced pepperoni,
chopped garlic, fennel seeds

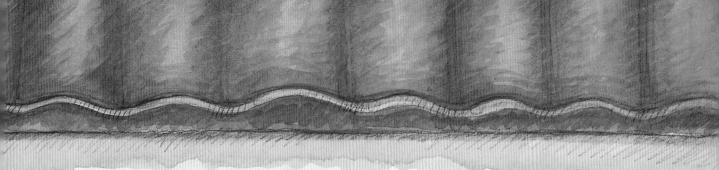

Dissolve the yeast in the warm water and let stand for 5 minutes. Combine the flour and salt. Add the yeast mixture and 3 tablespoons of the olive oil. Stir until flour is absorbed. Turn dough out onto a floured surface. Knead until smooth and elastic, adding more flour as necessary to keep the dough from sticking, about 2-3 minutes. Place the dough in a greased bowl, turning to coat. Cover with plastic wrap and let rise in a warm place until doubled in bulk, about 1 hour.

Preheat the oven to 425 degrees. Grease a pizza pan or a baking sheet. Punch the dough down and let rest for 5 minutes. Form the dough into a 10-inch circle on the prepared pan. Create little "hills and valleys" on the top of the dough by pushing dough apart in random places. Brush with the remaining 1 tablespoon olive oil and sprinkle with a topping (see previous page). Cover and let rise for 15 minutes. Bake 20-25 minutes or until golden brown. Cool completely in pan on a wire rack. Remove from the pan and serve.

Honey Sunflower Loaves

This bread makes excellent toast and can be shaped into rolls if you like.

2 cups water

1 cup rolled oats

½ cup honey

1 tablespoon butter

2 teaspoons salt

1 cup roasted sunflower kernels

1 (¼-ounce) package active dry yeast

½ cup warm water

2½ cups whole-wheat flour

2 cups white flour

Bring the water to a boil and stir in the oats. Set aside for 1 hour. Spray two 9 x 5 x 3-inch loaf pans with vegetable oil spray. Add the honey, butter, salt and sunflower kernels to oat mixture and stir well.

Dissolve the yeast
in the warm water and
allow to stand for 5 minutes.
Stir the yeast mixture into the oat
mixture. Blend in both flours, stirring
until the dough pulls cleanly away from
the sides of bowl. Form the dough into a ball
and place in a greased bowl, turning to
coat. Cover loosely with plastic wrap and
let rise in a warm place for 1 hour or until
doubled in size. Punch down the dough.
Knead until smooth and elastic. Divide into
two loaves and place in the prepared pans.
Cover and let rise again until doubled in size.
Preheat the oven to 350 degrees. Bake until golden
brown, about 45-50 minutes. If it appears that
bread is browning too quickly, cover with foil the
last 10-15 minutes of baking time. Remove bread
from pans and cool on a wire rack.

Makes 2 loaves.

Hawaiian Honey Bread

4½ cups flour

2 (¼ ounce) packages quick-rise yeast

1 teaspoon salt

½ cup milk

½ cup pineapple juice

⅓ cup margarine or butter

⅓ cup honey

1 egg

1 drop yellow food coloring (optional)

1 egg, slightly beaten, plus 1-tablespoon water

In a large mixer bowl, combine 2 cups flour, the yeast, and salt. Heat the milk, pineapple juice, margarine, and honey until very warm (120-130 degrees; the margarine does not need to melt).

Add the heated mixture to the flour mixture. Add the egg and food coloring, if desired. Beat at low speed until moistened. Beat 3 minutes at medium speed. By hand, gradually stir in enough of the remaining flour to make a soft dough. Knead on a floured surface until smooth and elastic, about 5 minutes. Place in a greased bowl, turning to grease the top. Cover and let rise in a warm place 15-20 minutes. Punch down the dough. On a lightly floured surface, shape into a round loaf. Place in a greased 9-inch pie pan. Cover and let rise in a warm place another 15-20 minutes.

Preheat the oven to 350 degrees. Combine one egg (slightly beaten) and 1 tablespoon water. Brush over the loaf. Bake for 35-40 minutes until golden brown. Remove from the pan to cool.

Makes 1 loaf.

Soft Pretzels

This is a fun recipe to do with children. It's a snack that is low in fat and sugar, which makes it an even better investment of your time.

1 (¼-ounce) package dry active yeast

1½ cups warm water

1 teaspoon salt

1 tablespoon sugar

4 cups flour

1 egg, beaten

coarse salt

Preheat the oven to 425 degrees. In a large mixing bowl, dissolve yeast in the warm water. Add the salt and sugar. Blend in the flour. Knead the dough until smooth. Form into twists or sticks. Place on a lightly greased cookie sheet. Brush the pretzel with the egg. Sprinkle with the salt. Bake for 12-15 minutes or until lightly golden brown.

Makes about 8-10 pretzels.

Apple Crisp Muffins

Some of you may remember the MacIntosh muffins from my bakery days. They were one of the most popular items we served. For those of you who would like the great flavor of that muffin without the coconut, this recipe is for you.

3½ cups flour

3 cups peeled diced apples

2 cups sugar

1 teaspoon salt

1 teaspoon baking soda

1 teaspoon ground cinnamon

1¼ cups vegetable oil

2 eggs, lightly beaten

½ cup chopped pecans

1 teaspoon vanilla

Preheat the oven to 350 degrees. Spray two 12-cup muffin tins with vegetable oil spray. In a large bowl, combine the flour, apples, sugar, salt, baking soda and cinnamon. Stir in the oil, eggs, pecans and vanilla. Fill the muffin cups to the top. Bake for 30 minutes. Cool on a wire rack for 5 minutes before removing from the pan. Makes 24 muffins.

Sunday Morning Muffins

These may become your "Sunday Best," in the category of muffins. Great for traveling and lunch boxes because they stay so moist.

2 cups flour

3/4 cup sugar

2 teaspoons ground cinnamon

2 teaspoons baking soda

1/2 teaspoon salt

3 eggs, lightly beaten

3/4 cup vegetable oil

2 cups grated carrots or zucchini

1/2 cup chopped pecans

1/2 cup undrained crushed pineapple

Preheat the oven to 350 degrees. Spray two 12-cup muffin tins with vegetable oil spray. In a large bowl, combine the flour with sugar, cinnamon, soda, and salt. In a small bowl, mix the eggs and oil and add to the flour mixture. Stir the batter just until the dry ingredients are moistened. Fold the carrots, pecans, and pineapple into the batter. Stir until blended. Pour the batter into the prepared muffin tins and bake 25-30 minutes or until a toothpick inserted into the center of a muffin comes out clean. Cool in the tins for 10 minutes before removing. Makes about 24 muffins.

Pound Cake Muffins

These muffins will double nicely as dessert. Keep several on hand in the freezer. Thaw and top with fruit and ice cream.

1 3/4 cups flour

1/2 teaspoon salt

1/4 teaspoon baking soda

1 cup sugar

1/2 cup butter or margarine, softened

2 eggs

1/2 cup sour cream

1 teaspoon vanilla

1/2 teaspoon lemon or rum extract (optional)

Preheat the oven to 400 degrees. Grease nine medium-sized muffin cups. In a small bowl, stir together the flour, salt and baking soda. In a large bowl, beat the sugar and butter with an electric mixer until well combined. Beat in the eggs, one at a time until well blended. Beat in the sour cream, vanilla and lemon extract until well blended. Beat in the dry ingredients until combined. Fill the muffin cups about two-thirds full. Bake 20-25 minutes, or until a toothpick inserted in the center of a muffin comes out clean. Cool on a wire rack for 5 minutes before removing from the pan.

Makes 9 muffins.

Connor's Lemon~Blueberry Muffins

2 cups flour
2/3 cup sugar
1 teaspoon baking powder
1 teaspoon baking soda
½ teaspoon salt
8 ounces yogurt
¼ cup butter or margarine, melted and cooled
1 egg, lightly beaten
2 teaspoons lemon zest
1 teaspoon vanilla
2 cups blueberries

Connor Agniel, one of Brooke's favorite buddies, loves blueberry muffins so much that he requests them in place of cake for his birthday.

This recipe was created for him!

Preheat the oven to 400 degrees. Grease twelve medium-sized muffin cups. In a large bowl, stir together the flour, sugar, baking powder, baking soda, and salt. In another bowl, stir together the yogurt, butter, egg, lemon zest, and vanilla until...

blended. Make a well in the center of the dry ingredients and add the yogurt mixture. Stir just to combine. Fold in the blueberries. Spoon the batter into the prepared muffin cups and sprinkle lightly...

with a little sugar. Bake 20-23 minutes or until a toothpick inserted in the center of muffin comes out clean.

Cool 5 minutes in the tin as is before removing to a wire rack.

Makes 12 muffins.

Happy Birthday!

SWEET CORN MUFFINS

There are as many different kinds of corn bread recipes as there are regions in this country. Every corn bread lover seems to have personal preferences. My preference is for sweet, golden yellow corn muffins. I love them so much, I even use leftovers to make croutons for salad.

1¼ cups flour

¾ cup yellow cornmeal

¼ cup sugar

1 tablespoon baking powder

½ teaspoon salt

1 cup milk

½ cup vegetable oil

2 eggs, lightly beaten

2 tablespoons butter, melted

2 tablespoons honey

1 teaspoon vanilla

Preheat the oven to 400 degrees. Spray a muffin tin with vegetable oil. In a large bowl, stir together the flour, cornmeal, sugar, baking powder, and salt. In another bowl, stir together the milk, oil, eggs, butter, honey, and vanilla until blended. Make a well in the center of the dry ingredients and add the milk mixture. Stir just to combine. Spoon the batter into the prepared muffin cups, about two-thirds full. Bake 15-20 minutes or until golden brown. Cool slightly before removing from the tin. Makes 6-8 medium-sized muffins.

Chocolate Chocolate Chip
MUFFINS

My children love these muffins.
They're great for any time of day and make
an excellent lunch box treat.

6 ounces semi-sweet chocolate chips

⅓ cup butter or margarine

¾ cup buttermilk

½ cup sugar

1 egg, lightly beaten

1½ teaspoons vanilla

1⅔ cups flour

1 teaspoon baking soda

½ teaspoon salt

6 ounces milk chocolate chips

Preheat the oven to 400 degrees. Grease twelve medium-sized muffin cups. In a microwave-safe cup, melt the semisweet chocolate chips with the butter, being careful not to scorch. Let cool about 10 minutes. In a small bowl, stir the chocolate mixture with the buttermilk, sugar, egg, and vanilla until blended. In a large bowl, stir together the flour,

baking soda, and salt. Make a well in the center of the dry ingredients. Add the chocolate mixture and stir just to combine. Fold in the milk chocolate chips. Fill each muffin cup two-thirds full. Bake 20-23 minutes, or until a toothpick inserted into the center of a muffin comes out clean. Cool for 5 minutes in the tin before removing to a wire rack to cool.

Makes 12 muffins.

Today's Special

Raisin Rye Bread

Each year when visiting New York City for the International Stationery Show, I had the pleasure of reuniting with my priceless friend, John Kalinski. He spoiled me rotten while I was there! To say that New Yorkers have created some of the finest restaurants in the entire world is not an exaggeration. This bread is as close as I can get to the recipe served at the deli near my hotel. I miss John so much, but especially when I smell this bread baking!

In a small bowl, cover the raisins with 1½ cups boiling water. Let stand while preparing the bread dough, then drain well. In a small bowl, dissolve the yeast in ½ cup warm water. In a large mixing bowl, place the ½ cup butter, brown sugar, molasses, and salt. Add the remaining 2 cups boiling water and stir until butter is melted. Add 2-3 cups of the flour. Beat with an electric mixer on low speed until combined. Then beat on medium speed for 3-4 minutes.

1 cup raisins

1½ cups boiling water plus 2 cups

2 (¼-ounce) packages dry yeast

½ cup warm water

½ cup butter plus 1 tablespoon

½ cup brown sugar

½ cup molasses

2 teaspoons salt

5½ cups flour

2 cups rye flour

Gradually add the yeast mixture and continue mixing. By hand, stir in the drained raisins, rye flour, and as much of the white flour as you can. Turn out onto a lightly floured surface and knead until smooth and elastic (about 7-8 minutes). Shape into a ball and place in a greased bowl, turning once to grease surface of the dough. Cover and let rise in a warm place until doubled in size (about 1-2 hours).

Punch the dough down. Turn out onto a lightly floured surface. Divide in half. Cover and let rise for 10 minutes. Shape each half into a round loaf and place on a greased baking sheet. Cover and let rise in warm place for an additional 30-40 minutes. Preheat the oven to 350 degrees. Bake loaves for 45-50 minutes or until the bread sounds hollow when tapped with your finger. Remove the bread from the pan and brush with the remaining butter.

Makes 2 loaves.

Cream Cheese Spread

1 (8 ounce) package
cream cheese, softened

1 tablespoon butter or margarine,
softened

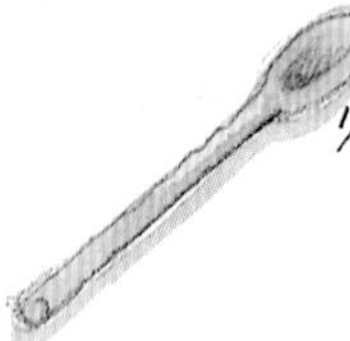

⅓ cup powdered sugar

¼ teaspoon vanilla

In a medium bowl, stir together all ingredients until smooth. Serve immediately or cover and refrigerate. To serve, let stand 15 minutes at room temperature to soften.

Makes about 1 cup.

A Grace Note

Blake
Last Morrow
Pup Cakes
Little Bit

Last Morrow
Pup Cakes
Little Bit

The list above is not a group of ingredients for some unusual recipe. If you could see my list in person, you would see a small piece of paper, so worn over time that it has the feel of velvet. The edges are torn and it has been folded and refolded so many times that I fear it may someday split in two. I've had this list since my oldest child, Blake, was just a toddler learning how to master the mystery of the English language.

Each word represents a word he struggled with ~ last morrow (yesterday), pup cakes (cup cakes), and Little Bit (his name for Elizabeth Sutton, a little friend with a big name).

Here's a list of my daughter Brooke's interesting words:

Bird Seeder (bird feeder)

Snow Puffs (ear muffs)

Kim O'Daddy Kelley
(her father, Kim O'Brian Kelley)

(continued on the next page...)

I kept a list of new words they had invented (to suit their purpose) in the laundry room, and as I waited for the washing machine to finish a cycle, I'd jot down some more. With each move we made, with each thorough cleaning out of drawers, I could never bear to throw the list away. It was such a sweet reminder of their innocence and a very special time in our lives.

I still love to listen to my children ~ they are much more articulate these days, I must admit. Listening intently has not always been my strong suit. I'm a self-confessed multitasker, and I have a hard time just standing still and really listening with purpose. This list from Last Morrow is my lesson in slowing down, and savoring each conversation I share with my children. For someday, when I long to run the brush through Brooke's golden hair or receive the gift of a spontaneous hug from Blake, I will have to settle for the velvety touch of the Last Morrow list... and some very sweet memories.

Brook
Bird Seeder
Snow Puffs
Kim O'Dados
Kelle

Soups & Salads

Chicken Cheese Soup

This recipe is from Joyce Schardt. Perhaps some of you who have purchased our earlier cookbooks recognize Joyce's name (aka: "Goose"). She is without a doubt one of the most talented people I have ever met, and also one of the most gracious. We have shared many growth experiences through the years and this book is just wouldn't be complete without a recipe from her.

2 whole chickens
16 cups water
10 chicken bouillon cubes
2 cups sliced carrots
2 cups sliced celery
1 onion, chopped
¼ cup fresh parsley, chopped
2 cups Minute Rice (uncooked)
1 (1-pound) can Rotel tomatoes
2 pounds pasteurized cheese

Simmer the chicken and water in a large stockpot with bouillon cubes until the meat falls away from the bone, about 45 minutes. Cool the chicken, reserving the broth. Discard the bones and shred the chicken. Add the sliced carrots and celery, chopped onion and parsley, Minute Rice, and tomatoes to the broth and simmer for 30 minutes. Add the chicken and cheese just prior to serving. Stir until well blended. Serves a crowd.

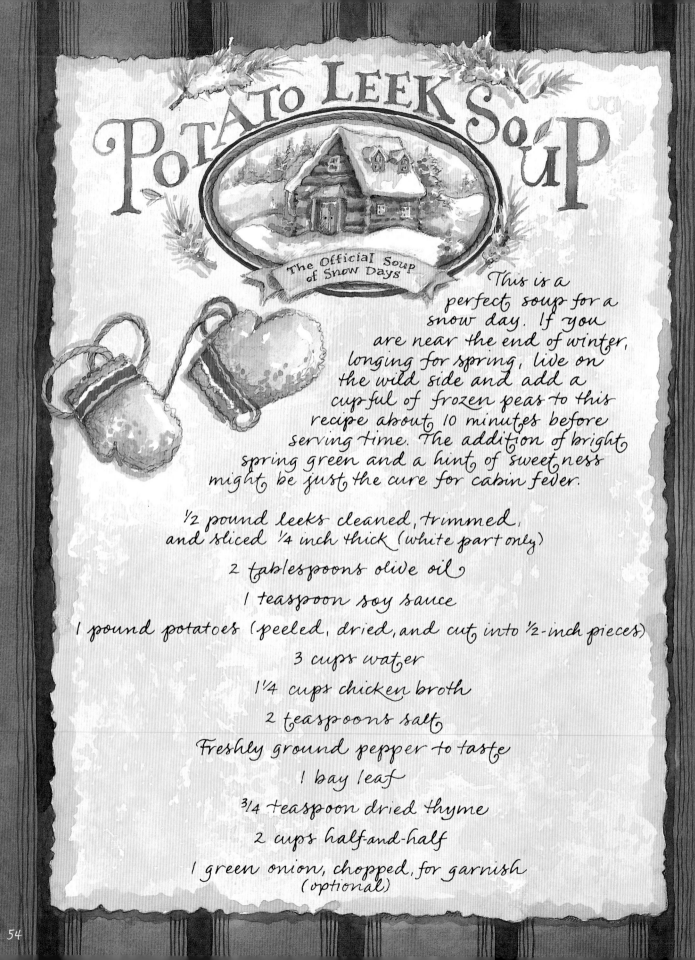

POTATO LEEK SOUP

The Official Soup of Snow Days

This is a perfect soup for a snow day. If you are near the end of winter, longing for spring, live on the wild side and add a cupful of frozen peas to this recipe about 10 minutes before serving time. The addition of bright spring green and a hint of sweetness might be just the cure for cabin fever.

½ pound leeks cleaned, trimmed, and sliced ¼ inch thick (white part only)

2 tablespoons olive oil

1 teaspoon soy sauce

1 pound potatoes (peeled, dried, and cut into ½-inch pieces)

3 cups water

1¼ cups chicken broth

2 teaspoons salt

Freshly ground pepper to taste

1 bay leaf

¾ teaspoon dried thyme

2 cups half-and-half

1 green onion, chopped, for garnish (optional)

Cook the leeks in
the olive oil over
medium heat for
10-15 minutes, stirring
frequently. Add the soy
sauce to the leeks after
they have begun to caramelize.
Continue cooking for a few
more minutes to make sure
the leeks are a uniform caramel
color. In a 3-quart pot, place
the leeks, their pan drippings, the potatoes,
water, chicken broth, salt, pepper and herbs. Cook over
medium heat until the potatoes are soft. Remove
from the heat, discard the bay leaf, and process
the soup in a blender to a coarse puree. Return the
soup to the pot. Whisk in the half-and-half.
Bring the soup to a gentle boil and immediately
remove from the heat. Serve at once, garnished
with the chopped green onion, if desired.

Serves 4-6.

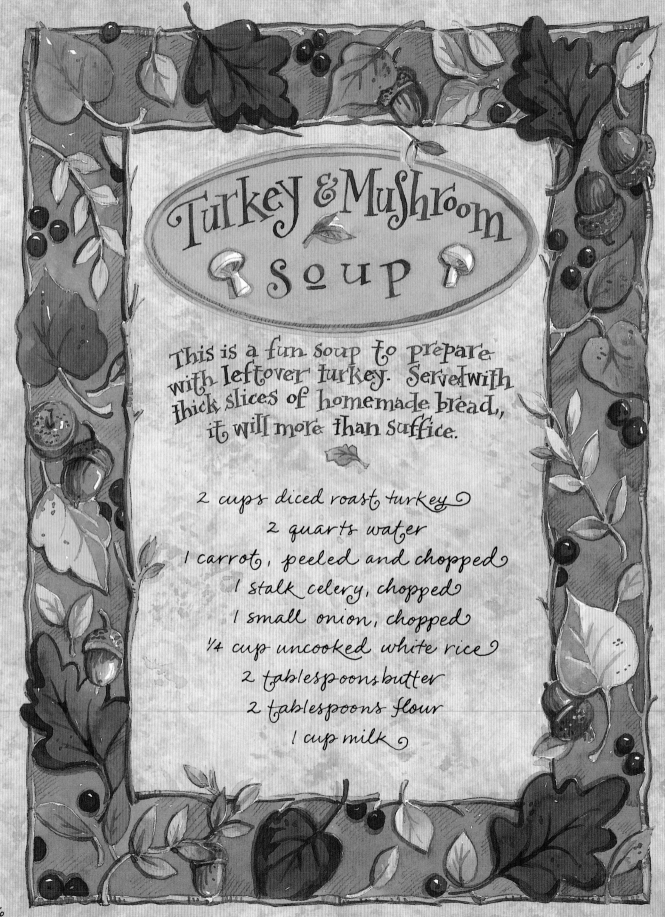

Turkey & Mushroom SOUP

This is a fun soup to prepare with leftover turkey. Served with thick slices of homemade bread, it will more than suffice.

2 cups diced roast turkey
2 quarts water
1 carrot, peeled and chopped
1 stalk celery, chopped
1 small onion, chopped
¼ cup uncooked white rice
2 tablespoons butter
2 tablespoons flour
1 cup milk

8 ounces mushrooms, sliced
1 cup half-and-half
Salt and freshly ground pepper
to taste

In a large soup pot, place the turkey, water, carrot, and onion. Simmer, covered, for about an hour. Bring the broth to a boil and add the rice. Simmer, covered, for 30 minutes, or until the rice is tender. In a small saucepan, melt the butter and blend in the flour. Gradually add the milk and cook until thickened, stirring frequently. Add the flour mixture and mushrooms to the soup pot and simmer for 5 minutes, stirring frequently. Add the half-and-half, salt, and pepper. Stir as you heat through and serve piping hot.

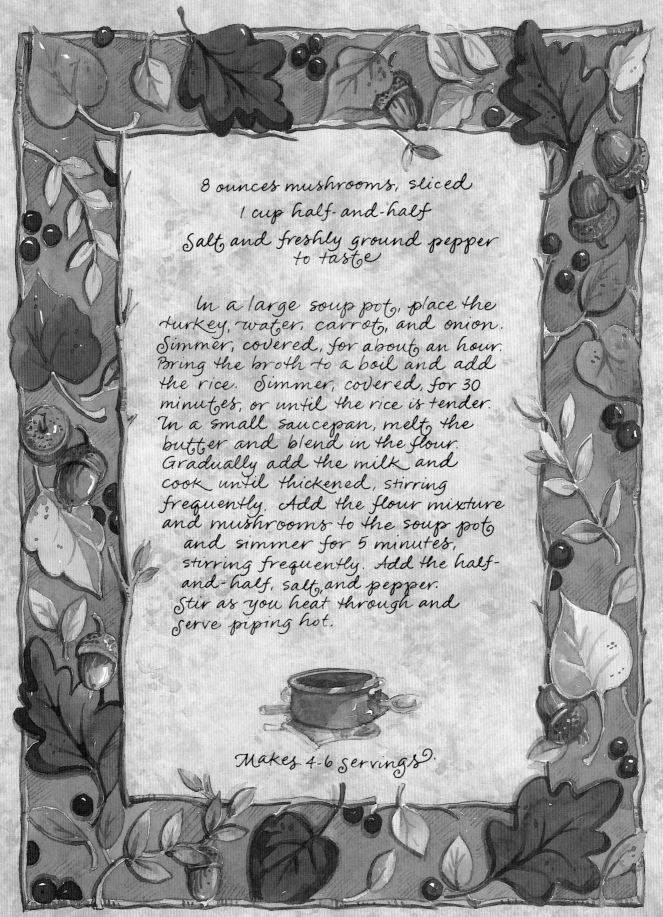

Makes 4-6 servings.

Corn Chowder

This is the kind of recipe that gets me into trouble with soup purists who look upon the convenience of canned soups with much disdain. So, if you're thinking about writing a letter to me about the use of canned soups, you might want to give it up. I shall not be moved

6 slices bacon

1 onion, chopped

2 (16-ounce) cans cream-style corn

2 (10 ¾-ounce) cans potato soup

2 cups half-and-half or milk

1 tablespoon snipped fresh chives

½ teaspoon thyme

In a large pan, cook the bacon. Add the onion. Sauté in the bacon fat until softened. Add the corn, potato soup and half-and-half, to pan. Stir until smooth and hot, about 10 minutes. Add the chives and thyme.

Serves about 8~10.

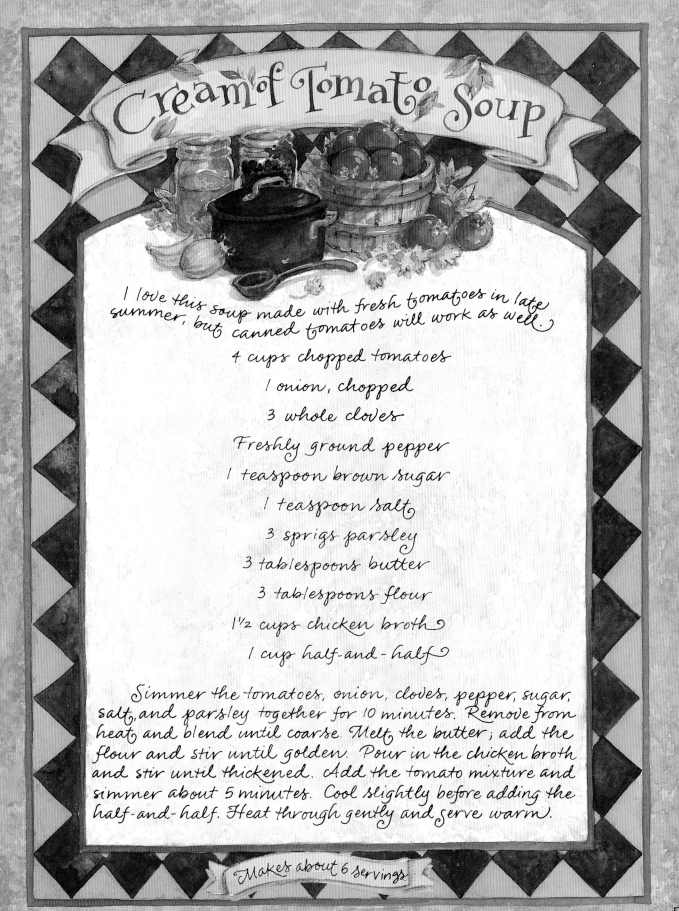

Cream of Tomato Soup

I love this soup made with fresh tomatoes in late summer, but canned tomatoes will work as well.

4 cups chopped tomatoes

1 onion, chopped

3 whole cloves

Freshly ground pepper

1 teaspoon brown sugar

1 teaspoon salt

3 sprigs parsley

3 tablespoons butter

3 tablespoons flour

1½ cups chicken broth

1 cup half-and-half

Simmer the tomatoes, onion, cloves, pepper, sugar, salt, and parsley together for 10 minutes. Remove from heat and blend until coarse. Melt the butter; add the flour and stir until golden. Pour in the chicken broth and stir until thickened. Add the tomato mixture and simmer about 5 minutes. Cool slightly before adding the half-and-half. Heat through gently and serve warm.

Makes about 6 servings.

Oodles of Noodles soup

This recipe is from my sister, Jan. Because she is such a great cook, I know you'll enjoy this soup. In addition to this talent, she is also a gifted painter, an awesome friend, and a wonderful source of spiritual nourishment.

1 (49½-ounces) can chicken broth

2 cups cubed, cooked chicken

½ cup coarsely chopped carrots

½ cup sliced celery

¼ cup chopped onion

1 bay leaf

6 ounces uncooked egg noodles

¼ cup flour

½ cup water

Salt and freshly ground pepper to taste

Minced fresh parsley for garnish

In a large saucepan, combine the broth, chicken, carrots, celery, onion, and bay leaf. Bring to a boil over medium-high heat. Add the noodles and cook until tender, about 10 minutes. In a small bowl, combine the flour with the water until smooth. Gradually stir the flour mixture into the soup; cook until slightly thickened, about 3 minutes. Season to taste with the salt and pepper. Remove the bay leaf and garnish with parsley.

Makes 8 servings.

Sweet Pepper Bisque

1 yellow onion, peeled and diced

1 clove garlic, minced

2 tablespoons butter

1 large sweet red bell pepper, seeded and diced

Dash hot pepper sauce

3 tablespoons flour

2 cups chicken broth

2 cups half-and-half

1 cup grated Swiss cheese

In a 3-quart saucepan sauté the onion and garlic in the butter until tender, about 5 minutes. Add the bell pepper and sauté for another 5 minutes. Then add the hot pepper sauce. Stir in the flour and cook over low heat for 2 minutes. Whisk in the chicken broth and cook over medium heat until the mixture thickens slightly. Puree in a food processor or blender until smooth. Return to the pan and whisk in the half-and-half. Heat through and stir in the cheese just before serving.

Serves 4-6.

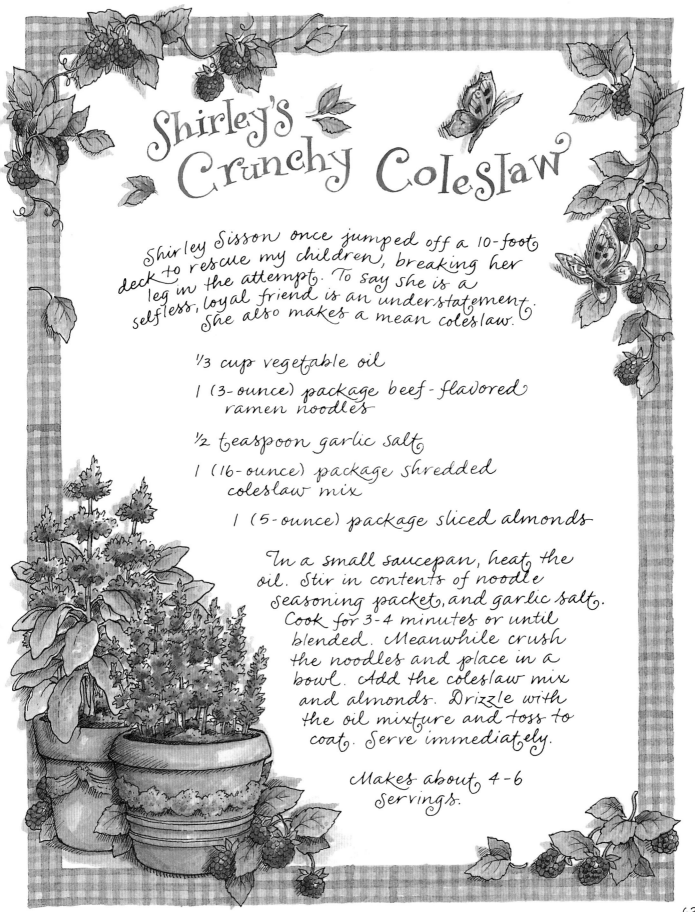

Shirley's Crunchy Coleslaw

Shirley Sisson once jumped off a 10-foot deck to rescue my children, breaking her leg in the attempt. To say she is a selfless, loyal friend is an understatement. She also makes a mean coleslaw.

1/3 cup vegetable oil

1 (3-ounce) package beef-flavored ramen noodles

1/2 teaspoon garlic salt

1 (16-ounce) package shredded coleslaw mix

1 (5-ounce) package sliced almonds

In a small saucepan, heat the oil. Stir in contents of noodle seasoning packet, and garlic salt. Cook for 3-4 minutes or until blended. Meanwhile crush the noodles and place in a bowl. Add the coleslaw mix and almonds. Drizzle with the oil mixture and toss to coat. Serve immediately.

Makes about 4-6 servings.

MISSOURI
Corn Bread Salad

This salad reminds me a little of the Southwest Sunburst Salad from page 68. Even though it's very similar, both are definitely worth including in this book.

Kansas City
Go Chiefs and Royals!

Our State Capitol
Jefferson City

Truman Lake

Keeping Good Co.

Lake of the Ozarks

St. Louis
Go Rams!
Go Cardinals!
Go Blues!

Suzan's House

Suzan and Ray on their way to KU to see their son, Jeff, play basketball! Go Jayhawks!

Serve in a large clear glass bowl if you have one. Thanks to Suzan Carey for sharing one of her family's favorites!

Bass Pro Shops Outdoor World

Home of Cashew Chicken
Go Bears!
Springfield
Branson

Dressing:

   1 (1-ounce) package ranch-style dressing
     mix

   1 cup Miracle Whip salad dressing

   1 (8-ounce) container sour cream

1 recipe corn bread, prepared from page 42

2 (15-ounce) cans whole kernel corn, drained

2 (15.5-ounce) cans red kidney beans, rinsed
   and drained

4 Roma tomatoes, chopped

1 sweet red bell pepper, seeded and chopped

1 green bell pepper, seeded and chopped

1 large onion or one bunch green onions,
   chopped

8 ounces shredded Cheddar cheese

10 slices bacon, cooked and crumbled

   Prepare the dressing using the
dressing mix, Miracle Whip, and sour
cream. Break half the corn bread
into a large glass bowl. Layer half the
corn, beans, tomatoes, peppers, onion, cheese
and dressing on top of the corn bread
and repeat with the remaining
ingredients. Chill until ready to serve.
Makes about 8-10 servings.

Janice's Macaroni Salad

Janice Steinmetz is a faithful friend from our "Among Friends" days. Just like her salad, she is a blend of many beautiful things.

Shelly Reeves Smith
2000

1 (16-ounce) package
   large macaroni shells

4 ounces fresh green
   beans

1 small cucumber,
   sliced

1 large ripe tomato,
   cored and coarsely
   chopped

½ cup cubed cooked ham

½ cup cubed cooked
   turkey

½ cup cubed sharp
   Cheddar cheese

½ cup pitted black olives,
   halved

Dressing:

½ cup vegetable oil

7 tablespoons red
   wine vinegar

2 tablespoons
   chopped fresh parsley

1 teaspoon dry
   mustard

½ teaspoon
   sugar

¼ teaspoon cayenne
   pepper

¼ teaspoon paprika

1 clove garlic, minced

Prepare the dressing by whisking together all of the ingredients listed. Set aside or store in an airtight container in the refrigerator until ready for use. Prepare the macaroni according to package directions. Drain and rinse briefly under cold water. Cook the green beans in boiling water until tender-crisp. Drain. Rinse under cold water. Cut into 2-inch lengths. Place in a large salad bowl. Add the remaining salad ingredients and toss with macaroni and dressing. Chill for at least 1 hour and serve. Makes 8-10 servings.

Southwest Sunburst Salad

This recipe was inspired by a salad
I enjoyed in a famous restaurant chain.
It was so refreshing and satisfying. You
can make a really fun presentation
with it by filling a huge shallow bowl
with the romaine lettuce and arranging
each of the remaining ingredients
radiating outward from the center
like rays of sunshine.

Toss tableside with the Avocado Ranch Dressing:

2 heads romaine lettuce, rinsed, dried, and chopped

2 cups sliced grilled chicken breast pieces (with or without barbecue sauce on the chicken)

1 cup corn, cooked, drained and chilled

1 cup cooked black beans, drained and rinsed

1 cucumber, peeled and diced

2 ripe tomatoes, diced

1 small can French fried onion rings

Avocado Ranch Dressing:

1 package ranch-style dressing mix

1 cup real mayonnaise

1 cup milk

1 (8 ounce) container of avocado dip

On the Side:

1 bag tortilla chips or one recipe Corn Bread Croutons (p.77)

Fill a shallow bowl with lettuce. Add the remaining salad ingredients as mentioned above. Surround the perimeter of salad with tortilla chips or Corn Bread Croutons. Toss tableside or pass the dressing.

Serves 8~10.

Thai Salad

1 small head green cabbage, chopped

1 small cucumber, peeled and diced

1 carrot, peeled and shredded

1 cup dry roasted peanuts, coarsely chopped

2 green onions, chopped

2 jalapeño peppers, chopped

Dressing:

⅓ cup vegetable oil

⅓ cup white vinegar

3 tablespoons sugar

½ cup chopped fresh cilantro

2 tablespoons salsa

3 cloves garlic, minced

½ small sweet red bell pepper, seeded and chopped

In a large bowl, combine the cabbage, cucumber, carrot, peanuts, green onions, and jalapeños. In a separate bowl, combine all dressing ingredients and whisk until well mixed. Pour the dressing over the vegetables and toss.

Serves 8-10.

Cucumber Salad

Light, sweet, and simple, this is a great little side salad!

1 cucumber, thinly sliced

½ cup diced sweet red bell pepper, or ¼ teaspoon red pepper flakes

¼ cup white vinegar

¼ cup water

1 tablespoon sugar

1 teaspoon salt

In a medium sized bowl, combine all ingredients and mix well. Cover and refrigerate for at least 30 minutes before Serving.

Makes 2-4 servings.

Oriental Chicken Salad

This is ideal for those moments when you're looking for something you can prepare a day in advance. The flavors blend harmoniously overnight and you're only 5 minutes from serving the next day.

Dressing:

- ¼ cup rice vinegar
- 2 tablespoons sugar
- 1 teaspoon salt
- 3 tablespoons sesame oil
- 1 tablespoon vegetable oil
- ½ teaspoon freshly ground pepper

- 4 chicken breast halves, skinned and boned
- 2 green onions, sliced 1 inch thick plus 1 green onion thinly sliced
- 1 (¼-inch-thick) slice fresh ginger
- 5 ounces Chinese noodles, cooked and drained
- 1 cup snow peas, sliced lengthwise

1 (8-ounce) can sliced water chestnuts, drained

½ cup sliced red bell pepper

¼ cup sliced almonds, toasted

1½ teaspoons sesame seeds, toasted

To make the dressing, whisk the vinegar, sugar, and salt until the sugar is dissolved. Add the oils and pepper and whisk until well blended. Set aside.

Place the chicken, the 2 green onions sliced 1 inch thick, and ginger in a stockpot and cover with water. Simmer until thoroughly cooked, 20-30 minutes. Drain, discarding the onions and ginger. Cool the chicken, cut into bite-sized pieces and place in a large bowl. Add the noodles, snow peas, water chestnuts, remaining green onion, and bell pepper. Pour the dressing over salad and toss. Cover and chill for 24 hours. Right before serving, sprinkle with the almonds and sesame seeds. Serves 4-6.

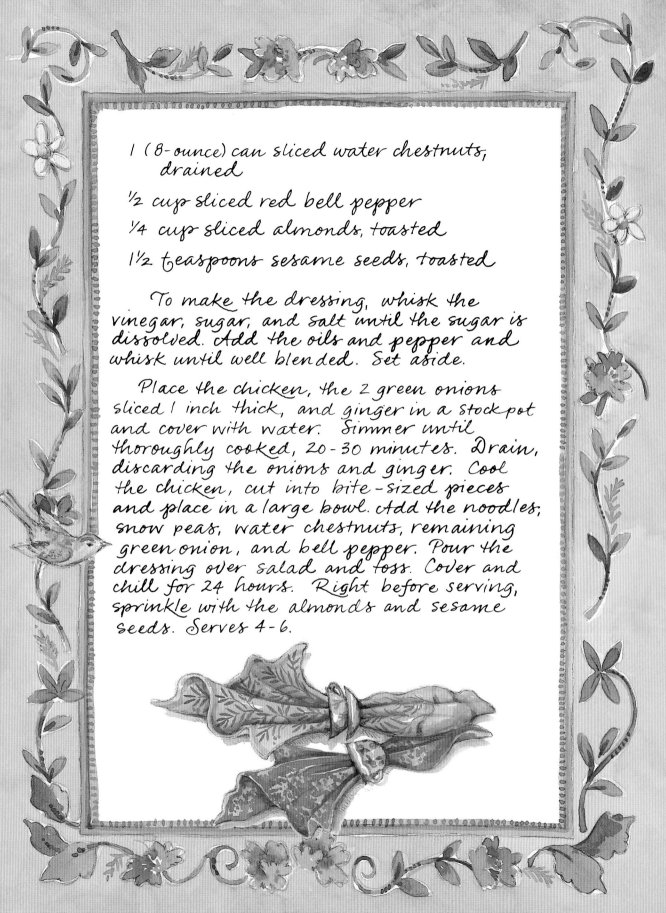

Pasta Salad

This is a year-round favorite for me.
I prepare it, using only vegetables and pasta.
Then, on the next day, I add grilled chicken to
the leftovers. You could add shrimp,
turkey, or salami as easily.

Dressing:

⅓ cup olive oil

¼ cup balsamic vinegar

Juice of ½ lemon

3 tablespoons Dijon mustard

1 teaspoon sweet basil

2 cloves garlic, minced

1 (16-ounce) package bow tie pasta

1 large onion, coarsely chopped

1 sweet, red or yellow bell pepper, seeded
and chopped

8 ounces fresh mushrooms, brushed clean
and halved

1 cup sliced carrots

1 zucchini, sliced

2 cups grape or cherry tomatoes, halved

Whisk all of the dressing ingredients together and store in an airtight container in the refrigerator. This dressing also works nicely on lettuce salads. While the dressing flavors blend, prepare the pasta according to package instructions.

Preheat the oven to 425 degrees. Spray a large baking sheet with olive oil cooking spray. Spread all the vegetables except the tomatoes evenly on the baking sheet. Spray the vegetables with olive oil cooking spray. Roast in the oven for about 15-20 minutes, turning once midway through the oven time. Then toss with the pasta and tomatoes. Pour the dressing evenly over top and toss gently. Serve warm or cold. Makes about 8-10 servings.

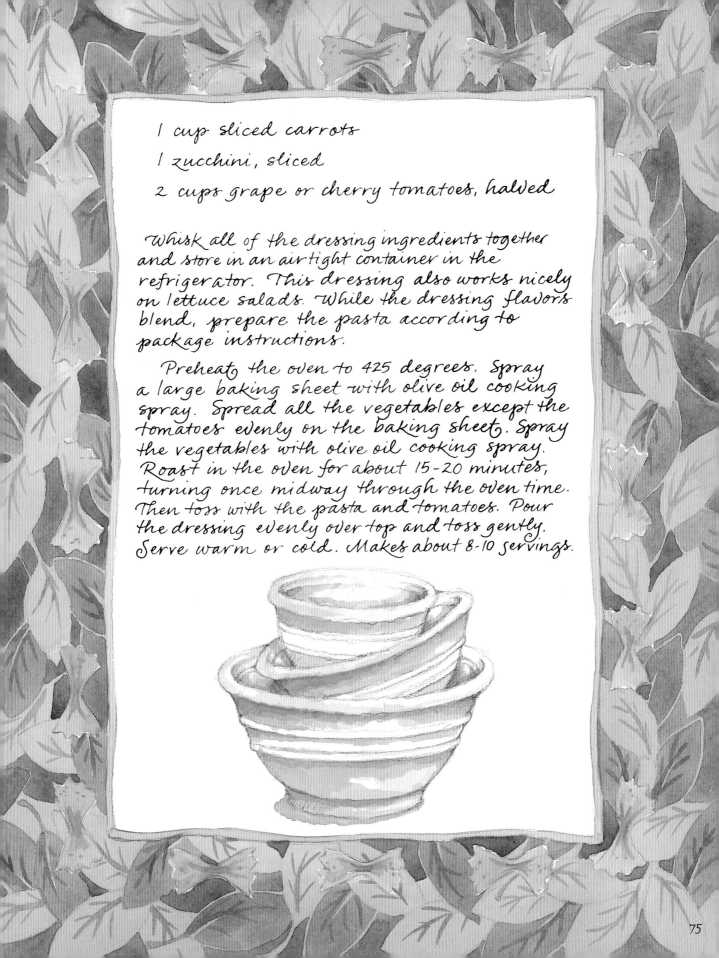

Tomato Basil Salad

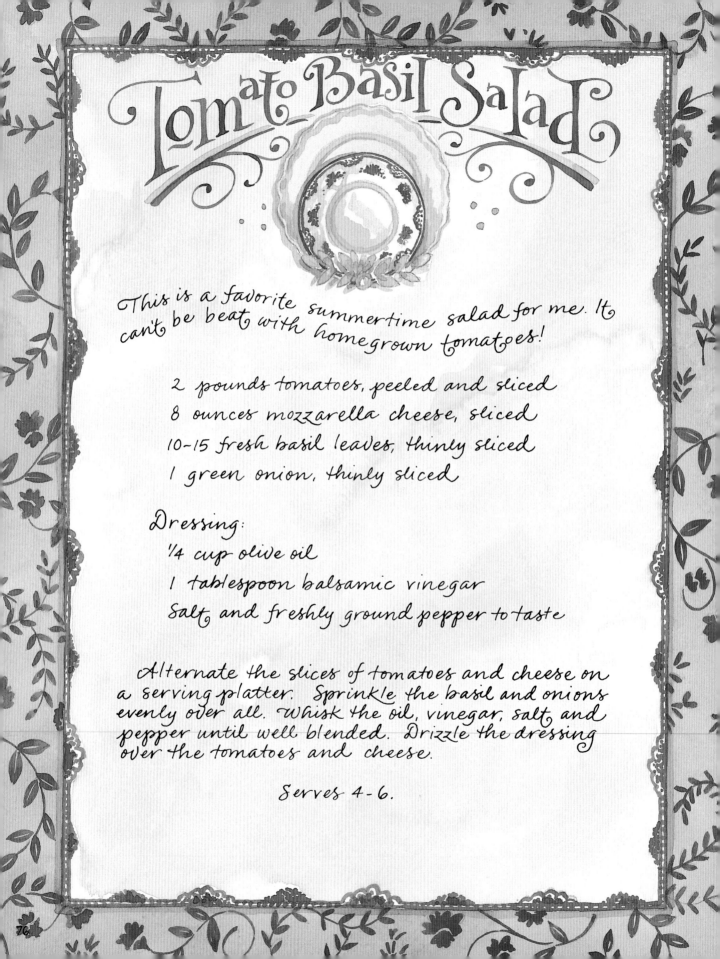

This is a favorite summertime salad for me. It can't be beat with homegrown tomatoes!

2 pounds tomatoes, peeled and sliced
8 ounces mozzarella cheese, sliced
10-15 fresh basil leaves, thinly sliced
1 green onion, thinly sliced

Dressing:
1/4 cup olive oil
1 tablespoon balsamic vinegar
Salt and freshly ground pepper to taste

Alternate the slices of tomatoes and cheese on a serving platter. Sprinkle the basil and onions evenly over all. Whisk the oil, vinegar, salt, and pepper until well blended. Drizzle the dressing over the tomatoes and cheese.

Serves 4-6.

Corn Bread Croutons

This is an excellent use of leftover corn bread. I enjoy these croutons on many kinds of salads and soups, but especially on those of the Tex-Mex variety.

2 cups 1-inch corn bread cubes

4 tablespoons butter, melted

Preheat oven to 450 degrees. Place the corn bread cubes in a large bowl. Drizzle the melted butter evenly over all. Toss gently. Spread evenly on a baking sheet. Toast in the oven for 4-6 minutes, turning once to brown evenly. Serve warm on salad or as a garnish on chili.

YUM!

Citrus Vinaigrette

Toss this dressing with field greens and garnish with Mandarin oranges. It's like a taste of sunshine.

½ cup water

2 tablespoons white wine vinegar

1 tablespoon cornstarch

1 clove garlic, minced

½ teaspoon salt

½ teaspoon dried sweet basil

½ teaspoon grated orange zest

1 teaspoon olive oil

Combine the water, vinegar, and cornstarch in a small saucepan. Bring to a boil and cook, stirring constantly, for 1 minute. Remove from the heat and set aside. Combine the garlic and salt in a bowl. Mash with the back of a spoon to make a paste. Stir into the cornstarch mixture with the basil, orange zest, and oil. Cover and chill at least 1 hour.

Makes
3/4 cup.

Pepper Cream Dressing

Try this dressing with any variety of lettuce and/or fresh vegetables.

1 cup mayonnaise
2 tablespoons water
½ teaspoon lemon juice
¾ teaspoon Worcestershire sauce
¾ teaspoon dry mustard
1 tablespoon freshly ground pepper
¾ teaspoon garlic salt
⅓ cup freshly grated Parmesan cheese

Combine all ingredients in a food processor fitted with the steel blade. Mix until well blended. Cover and chill at least 1 hour.

Makes 1½ cups.

A Grace Note

Recently my son was rushed to the emergency room after experiencing chest pains during one of his football games. After many, many tests, lots of prayer, an overnight stay, and a visit to a pediatric cardiologist in a nearby city, it was determined that his heart was healthy. The cardiologist took great care in counseling us, assuring Blake that he could go back to football ~ that he could go back to life-with-a-capital-L, that he shouldn't lose confidence in his heart or his health. The doctor said, "Don't live or play halfway because of this, Blake. You have a strong heart."

During the long drive home, I was thinking about how grateful I was that he was okay, and that the doctor took the time to explain to us how to carry on from that precarious place we were in.

Sometimes we have a tendency to associate gracious living only with gentleness and meekness. But living graciously also requires strength and courage. It means that even though we've been hurt or had a horrible scare, we are determined to find ways to become confident again that we can move through life without harm. We learn to trust that our hearts are strong enough to bear what comes our way.

Strong Heart Award
Blake Kelley

Main Dishes

© 2001 Shelly Reeves Smith

Brooke's TEX~MEX...

During the "experimentation days" for this book, my daughter claimed this recipe to be hers. It's a snap to prepare and although my audience was limited to people ages nine through thirteen, this dish got rave reviews.

1 large family size package chicken breast tenderloins, skinless and boneless

1 large onion, chopped

Seasoned salt and freshly ground pepper to taste

1 (4.5-ounce) can chopped green chiles

1 (16-ounce) jar salsa

2 cups shredded Monterey Jack and/or Cheddar cheese

Tortilla chips

Chicken Dinner

Preheat the oven to 350 degrees. Spray a 3-quart baking dish with cooking oil. Spread the tenderloins evenly over the bottom of the dish. Sprinkle the chopped onion over the chicken. Spray the chicken and onion with the cooking oil spray and season. Bake 45 minutes and drain off juices from chicken. Discard juices. Cover with the chiles, salsa, and cheese. Surround with the tortilla chips and return to the oven for an additional 7-10 minutes or until heated through.

Serves 4-6.

GRILLED Swordfish

Serve this with wild rice and a little fresh lemon on the side.

- 2 tablespoons soy sauce
- 2 tablespoons orange juice
- 1 tablespoon vegetable oil
- 1 tablespoon catsup
- 2 cloves garlic, minced
- 2 tablespoons minced fresh parsley
- ½ teaspoon lemon juice
- ¼ teaspoon dried oregano
- Freshly ground pepper and salt to taste
- 2 pounds swordfish steaks, about 1-inch thick

Whisk the soy sauce, orange juice, oil, catsup, garlic, parsley, lemon juice, oregano, pepper, and salt until well blended. Brush the marinade over the fish steaks; cover and chill for up to 4 hours. Grill or broil for 4-5 minutes per side, turning once. Serves 4.

SPINACH ALFREDO
Lasagna

This tasty recipe from Myra Pessina, busy mother of two, comes together quickly and easily.

12 ounces lasagna noodles

1 pound pork sausage

1 (10-ounce) package frozen chopped spinach, thawed and well drained

1 (17-ounce) jar Alfredo Sauce

½ teaspoon salt

¼ teaspoon pepper

1 egg

2 cups shredded Cheddar cheese

1 (15-ounce) carton ricotta cheese

½ cup grated Parmesan cheese

1 cup shredded mozzarella cheese

Soak the noodles in hot water for 15 minutes. Drain and set aside. Brown the sausage and drain. Add the spinach, Alfredo sauce, salt, and pepper to the sausage. In a bowl, combine the egg, Cheddar, ricotta, and Parmesan cheeses. Preheat the oven to 350 degrees. In an ungreased 9 x 13-inch baking dish, layer a third of sausage mixture, the noodles, and the cheese mixture. Repeat twice. Sprinkle with the mozzarella cheese. Cover and bake for 45 minutes. Let stand 15 minutes before serving.

Serves 8-10.

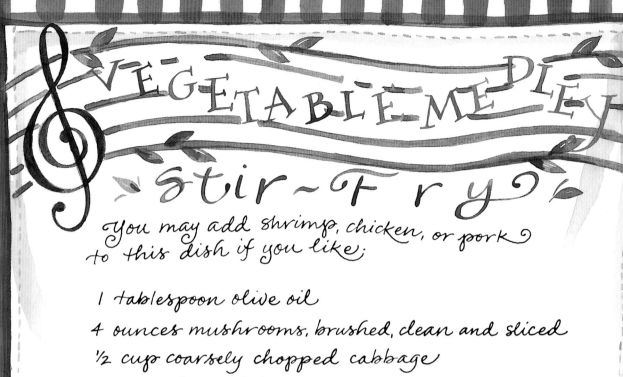

VEGETABLE MEDLEY

Stir~Fry

You may add shrimp, chicken, or pork to this dish if you like;

1 tablespoon olive oil

4 ounces mushrooms, brushed, clean and sliced

½ cup coarsely chopped cabbage

½ cup chopped broccoli

½ cup chopped cauliflower

½ sweet red bell pepper, seeded and chopped

1 small zucchini, sliced diagonally into
    ½ inch-thick pieces

⅓ cup water

¼ cup orange juice

¼ cup soy sauce

1 clove garlic, minced

2 teaspoons cornstarch

2 cups hot cooked rice

1 green onion, sliced

Heat the oil in a large skillet or wok over medium-high heat for 1 minute. Add the mushrooms, cabbage, and the next three ingredients. Stir-fry for 3 minutes. Add the zucchini and stir-fry for 3 minutes longer. Stir together the water and the next four ingredients until smooth. Add to the skillet, and stir-fry for 1 minute or until thickened. Serve over rice and garnish with the green onions.

Makes 4 servings.

CHICKEN POT PIE

1 (8.5-ounce) sheet frozen puff pastry

3 cups chicken broth

4 boneless, skinless chicken breast halves, cut into
1-inch pieces

3 carrots, sliced

6 red potatoes, scrubbed and sliced

1 cup thinly sliced celery

1 cup milk

⅓ cup flour

½ cup frozen peas

Salt and freshly ground pepper to taste

1 egg, lightly beaten

Place the frozen pastry on a clean, dry surface to thaw before unfolding. In a 3-quart pan combine the broth, chicken, carrots, potatoes, and celery. Bring to a boil and cook for about 5 minutes. In a jar, combine the milk and flour. Close the jar and shake until the mixture is smoothly blended. Stirring constantly, pour the flour mixture into the chicken mixture and bring to a boil. Reduce the heat to a simmer and stir until the sauce is thickened (about 1 minute). Stir in the peas. Season to taste with the salt and pepper. Preheat the oven to 400 degrees. Pour the mixture into a 9 x 13-inch baking dish. Unfold the puff pastry and place over the filling. Brush the top of the pastry lightly with the egg. Bake 10-15 minutes or until the pastry puffs and is a rich, shiny golden brown. Spoon into shallow bowls and enjoy.

Makes 6-8 servings.

"I will have mercy on you through my grace."

Isaiah 60:10

89

CHICKEN AMANDINE

HUGHES

Thank you to Kip and Debbie Hughes for sharing this recipe. Kip's sister, Jana, says this dish is a big hit with family members of all ages.

3 cups cubed cooked chicken

1 (10 ½-ounce) can cream of chicken or cream of mushroom soup

1 (8-ounce) can water chestnuts, sliced and drained

1 (4-ounce) can mushroom stems and pieces, drained

⅔ cup mayonnaise

½ cup chopped celery

½ cup chopped onion

½ cup sour cream

1 (8-ounce) package crescent roll dough

⅔ cup shredded Swiss cheese

½ cup slivered almonds

2-4 tablespoons melted butter

Preheat the oven to 375 degrees. Combine the first eight ingredients in a large saucepan. Cook over medium heat until hot and bubbly. Pour into an ungreased 12 x 8-inch baking dish. Unroll the crescent roll dough into two long rectangles. Place over the hot chicken mixture. Combine the remaining ingredients and spread over the dough. Bake for 20-25 minutes until golden brown.

Serves 4-6.

Camden County Catfish

Make sure the oil is hot, and the fish is very cold, and you should have no trouble with this recipe!

3 pounds catfish fillets

Chilled buttermilk

1 tablespoon dried crushed oregano

1 tablespoon crushed sweet basil

1 tablespoon lemon pepper

Seasoned salt to taste (or Bill Harper's Original Seasoning*)

2 tablespoons freshly grated Parmesan cheese

1 cup yellow cornmeal

Peanut oil

Place the fillets in a glass baking dish and cover completely with very cold buttermilk. Soak for at least 2 hours in the refrigerator. Combine the herbs and seasoning, Parmesan cheese, and cornmeal in a large plastic Ziplock bag.

In a deep skillet, heat the peanut oil to 375 degrees. Drain the fillets and place, one at a time, in a plastic bag containing the seasoning and cheese mixture, gently coating. Fry until golden brown and crunchy outside, about 2 minutes. Drain on paper towels and serve while hot. Serves 4-6.

* If you have trouble finding this seasoning, call 573-346-1779, Bill's company.

BAJA LASAGNA

For a new twist on an old favorite, try this dish which will feed a good-size crowd

16 (8-inch) corn tortillas

2 tablespoons vegetable oil

2 cloves garlic, minced

1 pound boneless, skinless chicken breasts, sliced into 2-inch pieces

5 (8-ounce) cans tomato sauce

1 teaspoon salt

Freshly ground pepper to taste

2 cups cottage cheese

1 (8-ounce) package cream cheese

1 cup sour cream

½ cup chopped Italian parsley

2 green onions, sliced

2 (4-ounce) cans chopped green chiles, drained

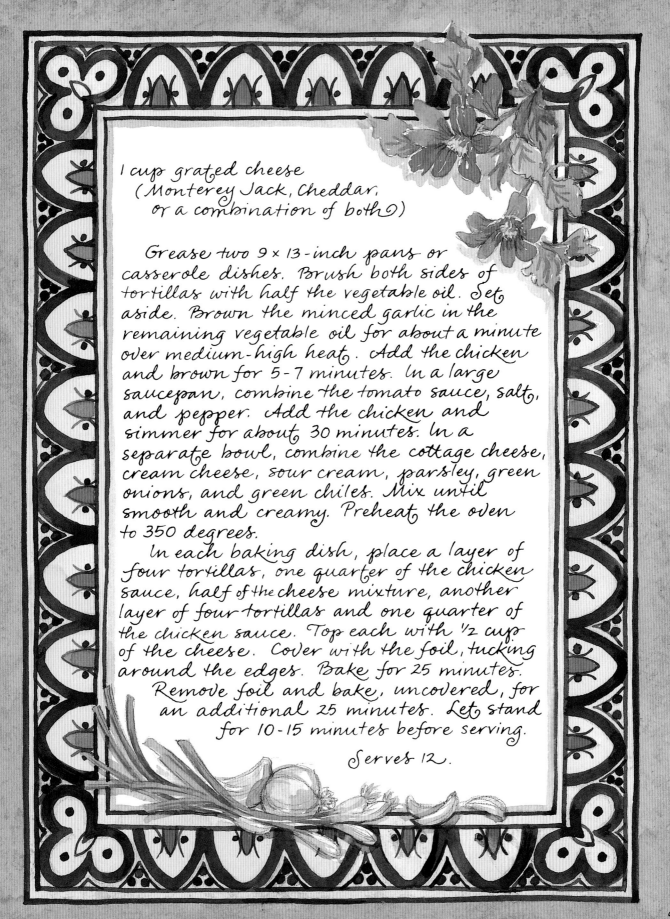

1 cup grated cheese
  (Monterey Jack, Cheddar,
    or a combination of both)

Grease two 9 x 13-inch pans or casserole dishes. Brush both sides of tortillas with half the vegetable oil. Set aside. Brown the minced garlic in the remaining vegetable oil for about a minute over medium-high heat. Add the chicken and brown for 5-7 minutes. In a large saucepan, combine the tomato sauce, salt, and pepper. Add the chicken and simmer for about 30 minutes. In a separate bowl, combine the cottage cheese, cream cheese, sour cream, parsley, green onions, and green chiles. Mix until smooth and creamy. Preheat the oven to 350 degrees.

In each baking dish, place a layer of four tortillas, one quarter of the chicken sauce, half of the cheese mixture, another layer of four tortillas and one quarter of the chicken sauce. Top each with ½ cup of the cheese. Cover with the foil, tucking around the edges. Bake for 25 minutes.

Remove foil and bake, uncovered, for an additional 25 minutes. Let stand for 10-15 minutes before serving.

Serves 12.

Donna's Pork Kabobs

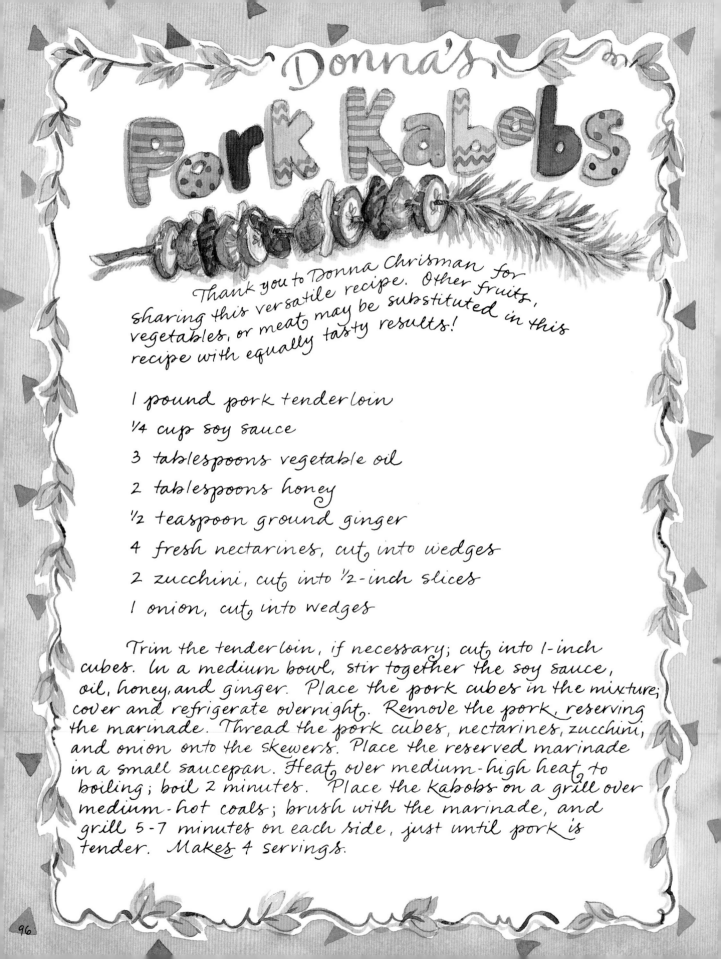

Thank you to Donna Chrisman for sharing this versatile recipe. Other fruits, vegetables, or meat may be substituted in this recipe with equally tasty results!

1 pound pork tenderloin

¼ cup soy sauce

3 tablespoons vegetable oil

2 tablespoons honey

½ teaspoon ground ginger

4 fresh nectarines, cut into wedges

2 zucchini, cut into ½-inch slices

1 onion, cut into wedges

Trim the tenderloin, if necessary; cut into 1-inch cubes. In a medium bowl, stir together the soy sauce, oil, honey, and ginger. Place the pork cubes in the mixture; cover and refrigerate overnight. Remove the pork, reserving the marinade. Thread the pork cubes, nectarines, zucchini, and onion onto the skewers. Place the reserved marinade in a small saucepan. Heat over medium-high heat to boiling; boil 2 minutes. Place the kabobs on a grill over medium-hot coals; brush with the marinade, and grill 5-7 minutes on each side, just until pork is tender. Makes 4 servings.

Fiesta Quiche

Try this dish with a nice Tex-Mex salad on the side, or Chicken Chili Stew from our third cookbook, <u>Keeping Good Company</u> published by Andrews McMeel.

Pastry:

You may use Norma's Piecrust recipe on page 154, or purchase a prepared 9-inch pie shell from the dairy section of your super market.

Filling:

5 eggs, beaten

2 cups milk

¼ cup salsa

½ onion, diced

1 (7-ounce) can chopped green chiles, drained

2 cups grated Monterey Jack and/or Cheddar cheese

Preheat the oven to 375 degrees. Place piecrust dough in a 9-inch pie plate. Crimp around the edges and prick bottom with a fork.

Combine the eggs, milk, salsa, onion, chiles, and cheese in a large bowl until well mixed. Pour into a pie shell. Bake for 35-40 minutes or until light golden brown and set in the center. Let stand 5 minutes before slicing.

Serves 6-8.

Blake's Baked Eggs

Isn't it interesting how much more fun it is to prepare a dish when you know it's a favorite of someone sitting at your table? I love making this for my son, Blake. The first time I played with this recipe, he took one bite and said, "M-m-m-m, can we have this again?" And so, we have!

6 eggs, beaten

½ cup milk

½ teaspoon dry mustard

¼ cup sliced green onion tops

1 cup chopped ham

1 cup shredded Cheddar cheese

Salt and freshly ground pepper to taste

Preheat the oven to 350 degrees. Grease a 7 x 9-inch baking dish.

Combine the eggs, milk, and dry mustard and beat well. Pour into prepared dish. Sprinkle onion, ham, and cheese evenly over the top of the eggs and bake for 25-30 minutes or until puffed and a knife inserted in the center comes out clean. Makes about 4-6 servings.

Note: Try Sunshine for Your Soul Veggies (page 116) with these eggs for brunch or dinner.

Skillet Dinner

Thanks again to Jana Agniel (Keeping Good Company Store Manager Extraordinaire) for sharing another one of her family's favorite recipes.

1 pound ground chuck, browned and drained

1 (15-ounce) can corn

1 (14.5-ounce) can diced tomatoes

1 (14.5-ounce) can carrots

1 cup water, if using fresh or frozen vegetables, not necessary if using canned vegetables

1 cup uncooked pasta

Dash chili powder

1 cup shredded Cheddar or mozzarella cheese

After browning and draining the ground chuck, add the corn, tomatoes, carrots, pasta and chili powder to the skillet. Cook over medium heat, stirring occasionally, until the pasta is tender. Reduce heat and simmer an additional 15-20 minutes. Top with the cheese and serve hot.

Serves 4-6.

Sour Cream Noodle Bake

Thank you to Diane Brennaman (another one of our gifted teachers!) for this recipe.

1 pound ground beef

1 tablespoon butter

1 teaspoon salt

1/8 teaspoon pepper

1/4 teaspoon garlic powder

2 cups tomato sauce

8 ounces egg noodles

1 cup cottage cheese

1 cup sour cream

1/4 cup sliced green onions

1 cup grated Cheddar cheese

Preheat oven to 350 degrees.
Sauté the beef in the butter and season with salt, pepper, and garlic powder. Drain. Add the tomato sauce and simmer for 5 minutes. Cook and drain the noodles. Add the cottage cheese, sour cream, and green onions to the noodles. Layer in a 2-quart casserole dish starting with the noodles and ending with the meat sauce. Sprinkle the Cheddar cheese on top and bake for 20-25 minutes. Serves 4-6.

Tomato Tart

A heartfelt thanks goes
out to Carol Zimmer for sharing this
recipe. This would be an ideal entrée for
brunch. Just marry it with a salad and some
fresh warm bread.

Pastry:

I suggest using Norma's Piecrust recipe on
page 154, or you may purchase one 9-inch pastry
shell in the dairy case at your supermarket.

2 tablespoons freshly grated Parmesan cheese

Tomato Filling:

2 tablespoons olive oil

1 medium onion, diced

2 cloves garlic, crushed

1 (28-ounce) can diced tomatoes, drained, juice reserved

1 teaspoon salt

Freshly ground pepper to taste

1 teaspoon sweet dried basil

1 teaspoon dried chives

1 cup mayonnaise
(regular or reduced fat)

1 cup shredded mozzarella
or Swiss cheese

Preheat the oven to 425 degrees. Fit the dough into a 9-inch pie plate or tart pan with removable bottom. Flute the edges of the crust and pierce the bottom of the pie shell with a fork. Sprinkle the Parmesan cheese over the crust and bake for 9-11 minutes or until light golden brown. Reduce oven temperature to 400 degrees.

Heat the olive oil in a medium skillet. Add the onion and garlic. Sauté until the onion starts to soften. Add the tomatoes, salt, and pepper. Add about ¼ cup of the reserved juice from the tomatoes to the skillet and bring to a boil. Boil for 1-2 minutes until almost all of the liquid has reduced. Stir in herbs and chives. Place the tomato mixture in the prepared pastry shell. Combine the mayonnaise and shredded cheese and spread on top of the tomatoes. Bake in 400 degree oven for 15-20 minutes or until the quiche is bubbly and cheese starts to brown. Let set 5 minutes before slicing and serving.

Serves 6-8.

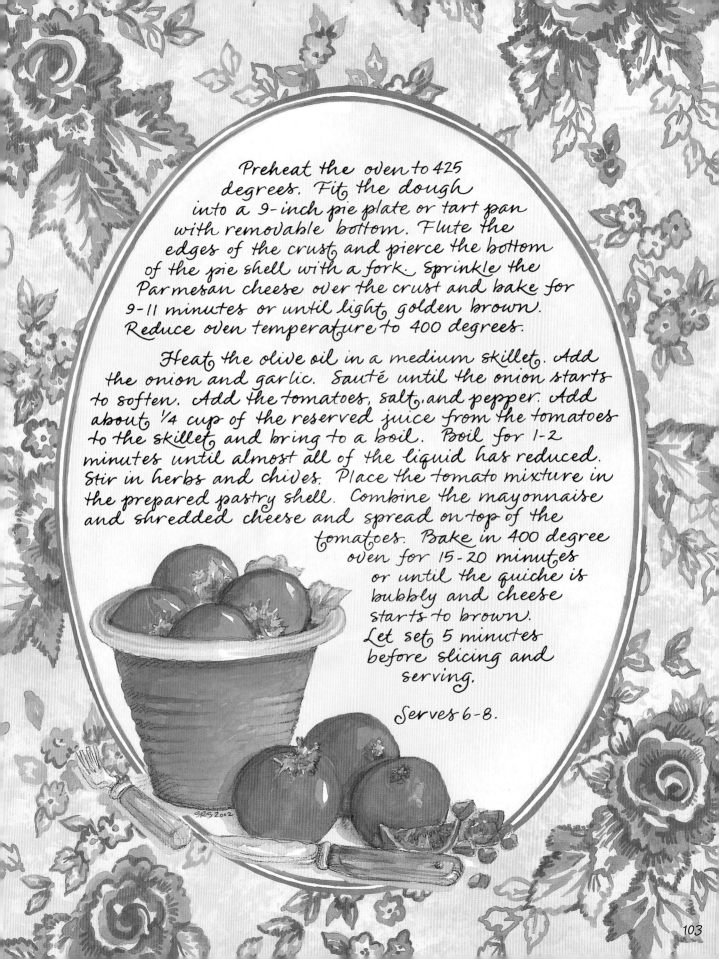

Schardts' Sauerbraten

Joyce Schardt prepares this for her "German husband" on his birthday each year. It requires several days to marinate in the refrigerator, but it's well worth the forethought and preparation.

2½ cups water plus ⅔ cup

1½ cups red wine vinegar

2 medium onions, sliced plus ½ cup chopped onion

1 lemon, sliced

1 tablespoon sugar

1 tablespoon salt

¼ teaspoon ground ginger

6 bay leaves

6 whole black peppercorns

1 (4-pound) boned and rolled beef rump roast

2 tablespoons cooking oil

½ cup chopped carrots

½ cup chopped celery

1 cup broken gingersnaps (about 8)

Hot buttered noodles

In a crock or a
large bowl, combine the
2½ cups water, wine vinegar,
sliced onions, lemon, sugar, salt,
ginger, bay leaves, and peppercorns.
Add the rump roast. Cover and
refrigerate 36-72 hours, turning the
meat occasionally. Remove the meat and
wipe dry with a paper towel. Strain the
marinade and reserve.

In a Dutch oven, brown the meat on all
sides in hot oil. Add the reserved marinade,
the chopped onion, carrots and celery. Cover
and cook slowly for two hours or until the meat
is tender.

Remove the meat to a warm platter while
preparing the sauce. Reserve 2 cups of the liquid
in the Dutch oven. Discard the rest. Add the
broken gingersnaps and the remaining ⅔ cup
water. Cook and stir until the mixture is
thickened and bubbly. Remove and
discard the bay leaves. Serve the
meat and sauce over the hot
buttered noodles.

Makes 8-10 servings.

Pork Chops with Apples

This dish is best prepared with a firm apple like a Granny Smith. Serve with a simple salad and Pam's Rolls (page 24).

4 pork chops, about 1-inch thick

Salt and freshly ground black pepper to taste

1 tablespoon olive oil

1 medium red onion, sliced

¼ head red cabbage, sliced

1 apple, peeled and cut into ½-inch thick slices

¼ cup cider vinegar

1 cup chicken broth

1 tablespoon sugar

Preheat the oven to 250 degrees. Place an ovenproof dish large enough to accommodate the pork chops in the oven to warm. The dish should have a tight-fitting lid.

Place the olive oil in a heavy skillet and heat over medium-high heat. Once the oil becomes hot, place the seasoned chops in the skillet and brown well, cooking about 1 minute on each side. Place the chops in the preheated oven-proof dish, cover tightly and bake for about 15 minutes.

Meanwhile, lower the heat under the skillet to medium. Add the sliced onion and cook until translucent, stirring occasionally for 5-7 minutes. Add the cabbage and apple and stir to combine. Add the vinegar and chicken broth.

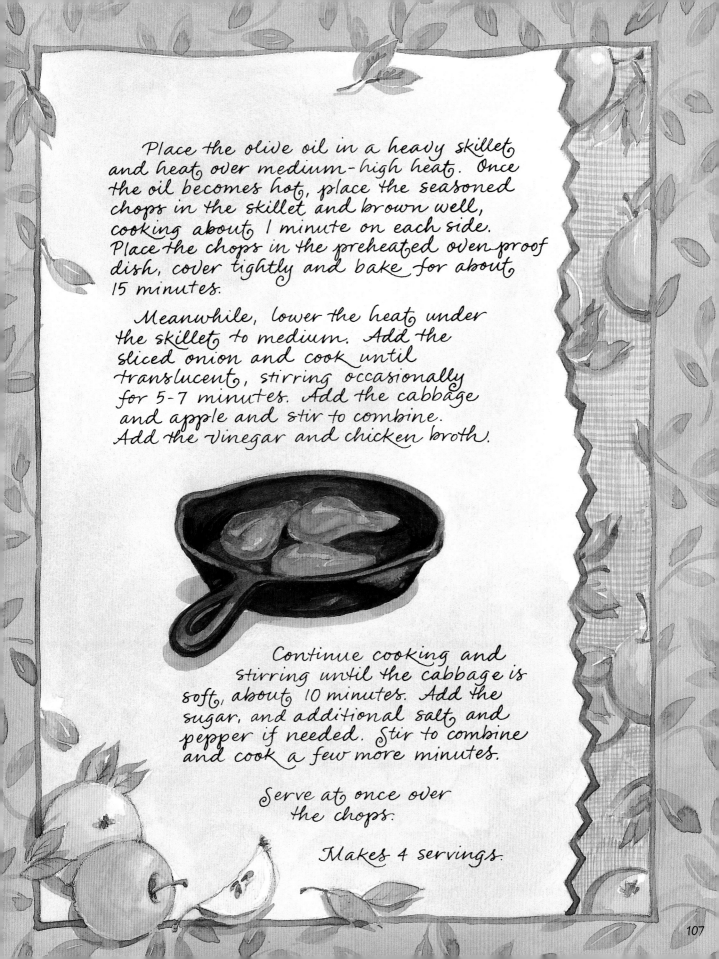

Continue cooking and stirring until the cabbage is soft, about 10 minutes. Add the sugar, and additional salt and pepper if needed. Stir to combine and cook a few more minutes.

Serve at once over the chops.

Makes 4 servings.

A Grace Note

Have you ever had a kitchen disaster? Why is it that these stories, when brought to mind, seem to grow funnier over the years?

Barring accidents that result in injury to someone, the combination of gadgetry, questionable sights, smells, and tastes seems to create a great setting for a Comedy of Errors.

I remember spilling sixteen egg whites over the top and down the sides of a kitchen cabinet once. Do you know how long it takes to chase sixteen egg whites around a kitchen until it's clean again? Then, of course, one would have to return to the store immediately to continue this particular recipe after this disaster, because no one has more than sixteen eggs in their refrigerator at one time, do they?

Gracious living means laughing at oneself (and at small disasters), and not being offended when others laugh with us, too. It means saving our hysteria for the big stuff. It means gaining perspective by placing oneself outside of the situation and witnessing it as if we were someone else looking on. It means admitting we make mistakes and that we don't always get it right the first time.

Keep smiling.

On the Subject of Side Dishes

     Writing this chapter is the most difficult one of all for me. I think I understand why. My favorite side dishes are like my favorite friends. They are simple, fresh, straightforward, and usually low-maintenance.

     We always believed that vegetables are most beautiful "in the raw" and the less we do to them, the better. So I naturally find it hard to mix them, mash them, or cover them with various sauces or cheeses.

     However, there are exceptions to some rules in our lives, aren't there? And so I share with you these fun recipes that will add some interest to our regular repertoire of "side kicks".

Royal Garden

Applesauce Snap

This extremely easy dish has only three ingredients, but it is so satisfying. It's chewy, crunchy, sweet, and snappy. You might add it to your menu the next time you serve pork chops or hot ham and cheese sandwiches.

3 cups applesauce

6 ounces sweetened dried cranberries

1 cup sliced almonds

In a small serving dish, layer the applesauce, then the cranberries, and then the almonds.

Chill until serving time.

Serves 6.

Oven Roasted Tomatoes

My children think they don't like tomatoes. I have tried the "but-you-like-catsup-and-pizza-and-that's-made-from-tomatoes" speech. They still insist they don't like _tomatoes_, as if this word italicized in their speech can't possibly be related to those foods. So many times I find myself on the brink of saying, "Oh, just wait, someday you'll appreciate the tomato for all it's worth!" But I don't say it, because I want them to have the pleasure of discovering this life lesson on their own, not because I nagged them into it. If I'm still writing cookbooks when they make this milestone in their lives, I'll share the moment with you.

Meanwhile, enjoy this tomato dish with me, won't you?

2 (28-ounce) cans Italian-style (plum) tomatoes

2 tablespoons sugar

A little more than ¼ cup olive oil

¼ cup butter, melted

Preheat the oven to 400 degrees. Drain the canned tomatoes, discarding the juice. Brush a small shallow roasting pan with a little of the olive oil. Place the tomatoes in the prepared pan. Stir the sugar, ¼ cup olive oil, and the butter together until combined. Drizzle over the tomatoes. Roast, uncovered, for 30 minutes, spooning the liquid over the tomatoes a few times during the oven time. Remove from the oven and transfer the tomatoes with a slotted spoon to a serving platter. Drizzle some of the juice from the pan over all and serve warm or at room temperature. Serves 8.

My Mom's Sweet Potatoes

Because my mom is such a great gardener, I brag about her green thumb all the time (a gift I did not inherit from her). She is also beautiful and funny and generous to a fault.

But her list of talents would not be complete if I didn't also mention that she is a very creative cook. This dish is a favorite of her friends and family.

3 cups mashed cooked sweet potatoes

1 cup sugar

2 eggs

½ cup milk

¼ cup butter, melted

1 teaspoon vanilla

½ teaspoon salt

Topping:

¼ cup butter, melted

1 cup brown sugar

½ cup flour

1 cup chopped pecans

Preheat the oven to 350 degrees. In a medium-sized bowl, combine all the ingredients other than those for the topping. Butter a 9 x 13-inch casserole dish. Mix well and turn into the prepared casserole dish. Mix all the topping ingredients together until crumbly and sprinkle over the sweet potato mixture. Bake, uncovered, for 30 minutes.

Serves about 6.

Sunshine for your Soul Veggies

You don't necessarily have to prepare this recipe only when your soul needs a lift. It can be enjoyed anytime. However, the cheerful colors and wholesome simple flavors of these vegetables always lift my spirits. This side dish can be served as easily with eggs as with any meat or poultry.

1 sweet bell pepper, red or yellow, seeded and chopped

6-8 small red potatoes, scrubbed and quartered

1 small red onion, chopped

1 pint fresh mushrooms, brushed clean and cut into halves

Seasoned salt and freshly ground pepper to taste

Preheat the oven to 425 degrees. Spray a large, heavy cookie sheet with olive oil. Spread all of the vegetables evenly over the surface of the cookie sheet and spray generously with olive oil. Season to taste and roast for about 20-25 minutes, turning only once during the oven time. The potatoes should be tender.

Serves 4-6.

Company Carrots

Mr. Rabbit

This recipe is worth the extra bit of trouble.

2-3 cups fresh julienned carrots

2 tablespoons butter

Freshly ground pepper and
    salt to taste

⅓ cup chicken broth

Sauté the strips of carrots in the butter for about 3 minutes. Grind fresh pepper over the carrots while they cook and season with salt to taste. Lower the heat and add the chicken broth. Cover and simmer until the carrots are tender, about 10-15 minutes.

Makes 4-5 servings.

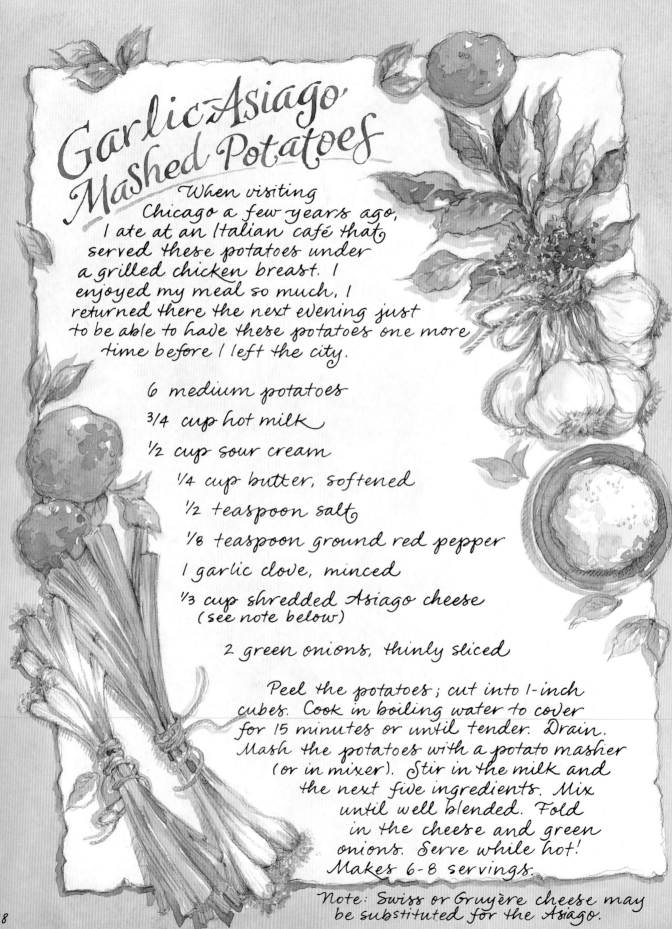

Garlic Asiago Mashed Potatoes

When visiting
Chicago a few years ago,
I ate at an Italian café that
served these potatoes under
a grilled chicken breast. I
enjoyed my meal so much, I
returned there the next evening just
to be able to have these potatoes one more
time before I left the city.

6 medium potatoes

3/4 cup hot milk

1/2 cup sour cream

1/4 cup butter, softened

1/2 teaspoon salt

1/8 teaspoon ground red pepper

1 garlic clove, minced

1/3 cup shredded Asiago cheese
(see note below)

2 green onions, thinly sliced

Peel the potatoes; cut into 1-inch
cubes. Cook in boiling water to cover
for 15 minutes or until tender. Drain.
Mash the potatoes with a potato masher
(or in mixer). Stir in the milk and
the next five ingredients. Mix
until well blended. Fold
in the cheese and green
onions. Serve while hot!
Makes 6-8 servings.

Note: Swiss or Gruyère cheese may
be substituted for the Asiago.

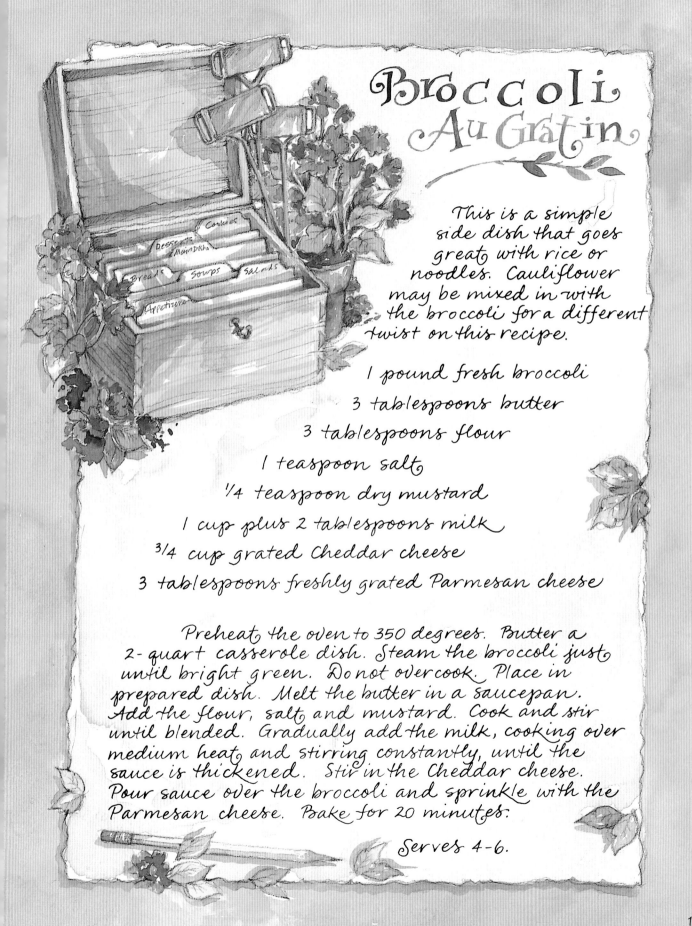

Broccoli Au Gratin

This is a simple side dish that goes great with rice or noodles. Cauliflower may be mixed in with the broccoli for a different twist on this recipe.

1 pound fresh broccoli

3 tablespoons butter

3 tablespoons flour

1 teaspoon salt

1/4 teaspoon dry mustard

1 cup plus 2 tablespoons milk

3/4 cup grated Cheddar cheese

3 tablespoons freshly grated Parmesan cheese

Preheat the oven to 350 degrees. Butter a 2-quart casserole dish. Steam the broccoli just until bright green. Do not overcook. Place in prepared dish. Melt the butter in a saucepan. Add the flour, salt and mustard. Cook and stir until blended. Gradually add the milk, cooking over medium heat and stirring constantly, until the sauce is thickened. Stir in the Cheddar cheese. Pour sauce over the broccoli and sprinkle with the Parmesan cheese. Bake for 20 minutes.

Serves 4-6.

Vidalia Onion & Rice

Casserole

This is oh-so-easy to prepare!

½ cup uncooked rice

1 cup water

5 or 6 Vidalia onions, sliced

¼ cup butter

1 teaspoon salt

1 cup grated Swiss cheese

⅔ cup half-and-half or evaporated milk

Prepare the rice according to package directions, using 1 cup water. Preheat the oven to 325 degrees. Butter a 13 × 9 × 3-inch baking dish. Sauté the onions in the butter until clear. Combine the rice, onions, salt, cheese, and half-and-half. Spread the mixture in the prepared dish. Bake for 1 hour.

Serves 6-8.

Home Fries

These fries remind me of my sweet grandmother. She used a cast iron skillet to fry them in and she seasoned with lots of salt! They're a nice accompaniment to brunch or breakfast.

6 cups cubed (1-inch pieces) potatoes

2 tablespoons vegetable oil

2 cups diced onions

Salt and freshly ground pepper to taste

Parboil the potatoes for 5 minutes, until barely tender. Drain well. Heat the oil in a heavy skillet and sauté the onions until clear, about 5 minutes. Add the potatoes and continue cooking. Brown on one side, then flip to brown the other side. Season.
Makes 6-8 servings.

Zucchini with Mozzarella

3 slices bacon, cut into 1-inch pieces

1 onion, chopped

1 clove garlic, minced

6 small zucchini, sliced

4 tomatoes, diced

2 teaspoons dried basil

1 cup tomato sauce

1 cup shredded mozzarella cheese

⅓ cup freshly grated Parmesan cheese

In a large skillet, cook the bacon until the fat is rendered. Add the onion and garlic. Cook until soft. Place a layer of zucchini slices in the pan, then a layer of tomatoes. Repeat the layering until the vegetables are used up. Sprinkle with basil and simmer, covered, for 5-10 minutes on medium heat. Turn the zucchini with a spatula so that the other side can begin to brown. Add the tomato sauce, and then top with the cheeses. Cover, turn the heat to low and simmer for 5-10 minutes, until the cheese is melted and bubbly.

Parsley   Thyme   Cilantro

Makes 6 - 8 servings.

Vidalia Honey Baked Onions

4 large Vidalia onions

1½ cups tomato juice

1½ cups water

2 tablespoons melted butter

2 tablespoons honey

Preheat the oven to 325 degrees. Butter a baking dish. Peel and trim the onions; cut each in half. Place in the prepared baking dish with the cut surface up. Combine the tomato juice, water, butter, and honey; pour over the onions. Bake for 1 hour or until the onions are soft.

Serves 6-8.

Garden Stuffed Potatoes

I can make a meal out of just this dish. Great any season of the year, these potatoes can be prepared ahead of time and warmed in the microwave.

4 russet potatoes

2 tablespoons butter

1 small onion, chopped

1 cup chopped cooked broccoli

½ cup ranch salad dressing

1 cup shredded Cheddar cheese

Kosher salt and freshly ground pepper to taste

Preheat the oven to 425 degrees. Pierce the potatoes and spray them with vegetable oil spray. Microwave for 12-15 minutes. Bake in a conventional oven for 15 minutes. Slice off the potato tops and scoop out the pulp, keeping skins intact. Mash the pulp in a medium bowl. Melt the butter in a small skillet over medium heat. Add the onion and sauté until tender, about 5 minutes. Add the onion, broccoli, salad dressing, and cheese to the potato pulp. Mix well. Spoon the potato mixture into the shells and season with salt and pepper. Place on a baking sheet. Bake the potatoes until heated through, about 15 minutes.

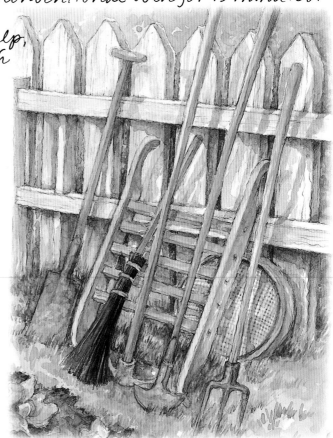

Serves 4.

Mushroom Casserole

I have a houseful of mushroom lovers, so this is a great dish for our family. If you're looking for an interesting recipe to serve with beef, this is it.

1 pound small whole mushrooms, brushed clean

6 tablespoons butter

2 teaspoons instant beef bouillon

½ cup hot water

2 tablespoons flour

½ cup half-and-half

Salt and freshly ground pepper to taste

½ cup grated Parmesan cheese

½ cup bread crumbs

Preheat the oven to 350 degrees. Grease a 9×9-inch baking dish. Sauté the mushrooms in 2 tablespoons of the butter; transfer to the prepared dish. Dissolve the bouillon in the hot water. In a saucepan, melt the remaining butter and blend in the flour. Slowly add the half-and-half, salt, pepper, and bouillon, cooking until smooth. Pour over the mushrooms. Mix the cheese and bread crumbs. Spread evenly over the mushrooms. Bake for 30 minutes.

Serves 4-6.

Dino's Potatoes

A warm thank you goes out to Jayne Wake for sharing this family favorite with me. It is nearly impossible... to describe Jim and Jayne without using the word "share" in some form! Their son-in-law Dino requested these potatoes so often that Jayne named them after him.

1 (10½-ounce) can cream of chicken soup

1 cup sour cream

8 ounces shredded Cheddar cheese

3/4 cup butter or margarine, melted

1 small onion, chopped

1 family-size bag of Tater Tots

6 slices bread, cut into cubes

Preheat the oven to 350 degrees. In a large bowl, combine the cream of chicken soup, sour cream, cheese, and ½ cup of the melted butter. Fold in the chopped onion and Tater Tots. Transfer this mixture to a 9 x 13-inch baking dish. Sprinkle the bread cubes over the top and drizzle with the remaining melted butter. Bake 1 hour.

Serves 8-10.

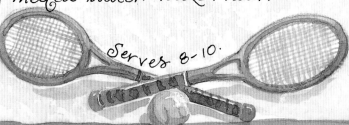

Monterey Rice

This layered dish is a great side for enchiladas or tacos.

3½ cups water

Salt, to taste

2 tablespoons butter

1½ cups uncooked long-grain white rice

1½ cups sour cream

1 (4-ounce) can chopped green chiles, drained

2 cups shredded Monterey Jack cheese

½ cup chopped sweet red bell pepper

Preheat the oven to 350 degrees. Spray a 2-quart baking dish with vegetable oil spray. Bring the water to a boil in a medium saucepan. Add the salt, butter, and rice. Cover, reduce heat, and cook for 20 minutes, or until water is absorbed. Place half the cooked rice in the prepared dish. Then layer half the sour cream, half the green chiles, half the cheese, and half the pepper. Repeat the layers.

Bake for 30 minutes.

Serves 6-8.

Mixed Grill of Seasonal Vegetables

Just because it's not summertime doesn't mean you can't enjoy a wonderful variety of grilled vegetables. In the dead of the winter, get out your stovetop griddle or one of the popular electric grills, and fill your kitchen with the aroma of nature's best seasonal offerings.

Fall/Winter Selection

Mushrooms   Potatoes

Onions   Butternut squash

Spring Selection

Artichokes

Asparagus

Garlic heads

Onions

Summer Selection

Tomatoes
Summer squash
Eggplant
Vidalia onion   Zucchini
Red, yellow, and green
sweet bell peppers
Red onion

Heat the grill until medium-hot. Lightly brush or spray the vegetables with olive oil. Cook until the grill marks are apparent, being careful not to overcook. Transfer to a large platter and serve. You may want to drizzle vegetables with a favorite oil, or season with favorite herbs after they have been grilled.

A Grace Note

The first image that comes to mind when I think of the word "gracious" is one of a hostess. But when we let ourselves ponder on what else that word could mean, we think also of those extraordinary people who seem to make every social situation a more pleasant experience for everyone involved, whether they are officially "in charge" or not. These gifted individuals can take a subtle lead (even during frustrating and confusing moments) and make everything seem bearable.

I've already mentioned our recent move to a new house. My sister, brother, and two of my nephews were kind enough to help move us on a rainy day in October. If you've ever moved in the rain, you understand how that <u>one</u> element of bad weather can add to the confusion. Among the things I couldn't locate for the next three days after the move were my cell phone charger, our cable for the television, and all of my underwear. Every flat surface in the new house was covered up with damp cardboard boxes and bubble-wrapped items of every kind. But set upon a nightstand in the bedroom all by itself was my Bible. I knew that my sister Jan had not only placed it there but in all likelihood, she had pushed everything else around it out of range so that it could be easily seen. Jan was our "moving hostess", silently providing us with one of the tools of grace we would need over the upcoming days. Isn't it nice that quiet lessons in living graciously are alive through people like this?

"May the grace of our Savior... rest upon us from above."
—John Newton 1779

Desserts

© 2001 Shelly Reeves Smith

Cream Cheese Pound Cake

I know that the ingredients listed for this cake are a dieter's nightmare. But it is so scrumptious! Consider this ~ you will only need the thinnest of slices to be satisfied.

1 cup butter at room temperature

1 (8-ounce) package cream cheese, at room temperature

3 cups sugar

6 eggs

3 cups sifted cake flour

2 teaspoons vanilla

Grease a 10-inch tube pan. In a mixer, combine the butter and cream cheese and beat on low speed until well mixed. Add the sugar gradually and beat until light and fluffy. Beat in the eggs, one at a time, beating well after each addition. Add the flour and vanilla, and beat only until the flour disappears. Pour the mixture into the prepared pan. Place in a cold oven, and turn the oven temperature to 325 degrees. Bake the cake for 1 hour and 10 minutes. Cool on a wire rack and chill before serving. Freezes well.

Serves 12-15.

Pumpkin Cheesecake Tarts

This dessert is especially nice in the fall. For a fun presentation, place a layer of paper fall leaves on the serving platter under the tarts.

12 paper muffin cup liners

12 gingersnap cookies

1 (8-ounce) package cream cheese, softened

1 cup solid-pack pumpkin

½ cup sugar

1 teaspoon pumpkin pie spice

1 teaspoon vanilla

2 eggs

Preheat the oven to 325 degrees. Place the muffin cup liners in a muffin tin. Place a gingersnap cookie in the bottom of each liner. Beat cream cheese, pumpkin sugar, pumpkin pie spice, and vanilla until well blended. Add the eggs and beat well. Divide the batter equally among the 12 muffin cups. Bake for 20-25 minutes or until set. Cool in the pan on a wire rack. Remove from the pan and chill before serving.

Makes 12.

Buttery Streusel Coffee Cake

Many of you will remember Dee Stoelting's recipes from our other cookbooks. She has a reputation in our community for being not only an excellent cook but for presenting food in such a beautiful way as well. So much love and creativity go into each dish she prepares. Dee made this coffee cake for my family after we helped cater her daughter's wedding. We ate every crumb.

Dough:

    3 cups flour

    1½ cups sugar

    1 tablespoon plus 2 teaspoons baking powder

    1½ teaspoons salt

    ½ cup margarine or butter

    1½ cups milk

    2 eggs

Cinnamon Nut Filling

    ½ cup brown sugar

    ½ cup finely chopped pecans

    2 teaspoons ground cinnamon

Streusel Topping

    ½ cup flour

    1 cup sugar

    ½ cup firm butter

Glaze

2 cups powdered sugar
1/4 cup butter, softened
1 teaspoon vanilla
1/3 - 1/2 cup water

Preheat the oven to 375 degrees. Spray two 9-inch square cake pans with vegetable oil spray. Mix all the dough ingredients together until moist and beat 1 minute. Spread one quarter of the batter in each prepared pan. Mix the filling ingredients together. Divide the Cinnamon Nut Filling in half and sprinkle over the cake layer in each pan. Then divide the remaining batter between each pan. Prepare the Streusel Topping. Mix together all the topping ingredients until crumbly and divide between the two pans. Bake 30-35 minutes or until a toothpick inserted in the center comes out clean.

Meanwhile, beat the powdered sugar and butter together until creamy. Add the vanilla and mix well. Add the water as needed, a tablespoon at a time, to make a drizzle consistency. Drizzle the baked cakes with glaze while warm. Serves 10-12.

Dee's Blueberry-Lemon Cheesecake

Another stupendous recipe from Dee Stoelting! Imagine this light and luscious cheesecake served on periwinkle dessert plates, garnished with pansies (grown from seed by Dee) and homemade lemonade on the side! That's how Dee presented this dish to us one evening last summer.

Crust:

1½ cups finely ground almonds

¼ cup sugar

3 tablespoons softened butter

1 tablespoon flour

Filling:

3 (8-ounce) packages cream cheese, softened

1¼ cups sugar

3 tablespoons flour

½ teaspoon salt

4 large eggs

8 ounces sour cream

1 teaspoon vanilla

1 tablespoon lemon zest

1 2/3 cups fresh or frozen blueberries

Topping:

1 cup whipping cream

2 teaspoons sugar

2 tablespoons sour cream

Preheat the oven to 300 degrees. Lightly grease a 9-inch springform pan. In a small bowl, combine crust ingredients. Press the mixture into the bottom and 1 1/2-inches up the sides of the prepared pan; set aside.

(continued on the next page...)

Beat the cream cheese at medium
speed with an electric mixer until smooth.
Combine 1¼ cups sugar, 3 tablespoons
flour and the salt. Add to the cream cheese,
beating until blended. Add the eggs, one
at a time beating well after each addition.
Add the 8 ounces sour cream, vanilla, and
lemon zest, beating just until blended.
Gently fold in the berries. Pour the mixture
into the prepared
pan. Warning!
The pan will

be very full! Bake
1 hour and 10 minutes or until set. Turn
off the oven and let the cheesecake stand
in oven with the door partially open for
30 minutes. Remove the cheesecake from
the oven. Cool in the pan on a wire rack
for 30 minutes. Cover and chill 8 hours.
Release the sides of the pan. Prepare the
topping by whipping cream at high speed
until foamy, gradually adding 2 teaspoons
sugar, beating until stiff peaks form.
Fold in 2 tablespoons sour cream. Spread
over the cheesecake.

Serves 10-12.

Myra's Rich Chocolate Chip Cheese Bars

She's not kidding about the rich part.

2 cups chocolate chip cookie dough, or 1 (18-ounce) package refrigerated dough

1 (8-ounce) package cream cheese, softened

2/3 cup sugar

1 egg

Preheat the oven to 350 degrees. Press half the cookie dough in the bottom of an 8-inch square pan. Beat the cream cheese, sugar, and egg until smooth. Spread over the cookie dough. Sprinkle the remaining cookie dough over the cream cheese mixture. Bake for 30-35 minutes. Serve chilled.

Makes 8-10 servings.

White Texas Cake

Most of us have tried Texas sheet cake before ~ a wonderfully rich chocolate cake topped off with a chocolate glaze. Carolyn Miller's recipe for White Texas Cake is the tasty opposite. It is especially appropriate for Carolyn to be featured in this book, since I consider her to be one of the most gracious people I know.

⅓ cup shortening

2 egg whites

2 cups sugar

1 teaspoon baking soda

1 teaspoon salt

2 cups flour

1¾ cup buttermilk

1 teaspoon vanilla

½ teaspoon almond flavoring

Icing:

½ cup margarine or butter, melted
½ cup flaked coconut
⅓ cup buttermilk
2½ cups powdered sugar

Preheat the oven to 350 degrees. Grease and flour a 10 × 15-inch pan. In a mixer, beat first three ingredients together. Add baking soda, salt, flour, buttermilk, vanilla, and almond flavoring. Beat on medium speed for about 2 minutes.

Pour the batter into the prepared pan and bake 25-30 minutes or until light golden brown.

In a mixer, combine all icing ingredients and blend until smooth. Top with the icing while the cake is warm.

Serves
12-15.

Margie's Cherry DESSERT

This recipe is from "Grandma Margie". She's not my grandma. But, that's how we all know her! Thanks to her daughter, Marcheta, for sharing.

Crust:

3 cups graham cracker crumbs

½ cup sugar

4 tablespoons butter or margarine

Filling:

1 (8-ounce) package cream cheese, softened

2 (14-ounce) cans sweetened condensed milk

Juice of 1 lemon

Topping:

1 (21-ounce) can cherry pie filling

Preheat the oven to 300 degrees. Sprinkle the graham cracker crumbs in the bottom of a 9 × 13-inch baking pan. Sprinkle the sugar over this and then slice the butter

over the top of all this. Bake until the butter has melted and the crust is light brown. Stir with a fork and spread out evenly. Let cool.

Mix the filling ingredients together until thickened and spread on to the cooled crust. Refrigerate until filling is chilled. Spread the topping evenly over all and serve.

Serves 12.

Peanut Butter Cup Cookies

For a serious sweet tooth, these cookies will not disappoint you.

2 1/4 cups flour

1/3 cup cocoa

1 teaspoon baking soda

1/2 teaspoon salt

1 cup butter

3/4 cup smooth peanut butter

3/4 cup packed brown sugar

3/4 cup granulated sugar

1 teaspoon vanilla

2 eggs

10 ounces peanut butter cups, coarsely chopped

1 cup (6 ounces) semi-sweet chocolate chips

Preheat the oven to 350 degrees. Combine the flour, cocoa, baking soda, and salt. In a large bowl, beat the butter, peanut butter, sugars, and vanilla until light and fluffy. Add the eggs, one at a time, beating well after each addition until thoroughly blended. Stir in the dry ingredients until smooth. Fold in the peanut butter cups and chocolate chips. Spoon 2 tablespoons dough about 2 inches apart onto an ungreased baking sheet. Bake until slightly firm to the touch, but not brown, 10-13 minutes. Cool for a few minutes before transferring from the baking sheet to a wire rack to cool completely.

Makes about 3 dozen.

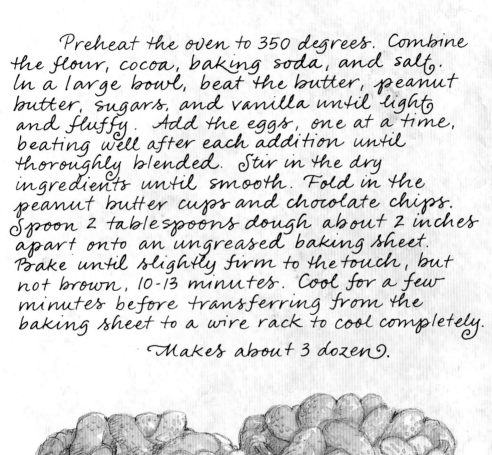

18-Karat Gold Neighbor Cake

It's difficult to say just how valuable a good neighbor is. When we put our house on the market this past year, I was tempted to list on the sell sheet, along with all of the other fine qualities of our house, "Million Dollar Neighbors!" This recipe was created for the Feine family. Gary loves carrot cake, so this was my meager attempt to say thank you for all the countless ways Gary and Carla helped make my life a little easier on Oak Tree Road. You may bake this in two 9-inch cake pans or 6 miniature loaf pans (enough to share with all your wonderful neighbors).

2 cups flour

2 cups sugar

2 teaspoons ground cinnamon

½ teaspoon nutmeg

1 teaspoon salt

1 cup butter, melted

½ cup vegetable oil

4 eggs, beaten

3 cups grated carrots

Cream Cheese Frosting:

1 (8-ounce) package cream cheese, softened

½ cup butter, softened

1 teaspoon vanilla

5 cups powdered sugar

Preheat the oven to 350 degrees. Spray the baking pans with cooking oil. In a mixing bowl, combine the flour, sugar, cinnamon, nutmeg and salt. Add the butter, vegetable oil, eggs, and carrots. Beat for 2 minutes on medium speed. Pour the batter into the prepared pans and bake 20-35 minutes, depending on the size of the pans. The cakes are done when a toothpick inserted in the center comes out clean.

Meanwhile, prepare the frosting. In a mixing bowl, combine all ingredients and beat at medium to high speed for 2-4 minutes, scraping down the sides of the bowl often to prevent lumps. Frost cake after it has cooled completely.

Serves 10-12.

Cream Cheese Cupcakes

This dessert is one of my daughter's favorites. It comes from the mother of a former classmate of Brooke's, Jared Danangelis. Even though Jared has moved far away, he will always be close to Brooke's heart!

1 (1 pound, 2.25 ounce) box chocolate cake mix, batter prepared according to directions on package but not baked

24 cupcake liners

Filling:

1 (8-ounce) package cream cheese, softened

1 egg

1/3 cup sugar

Dash of salt

12 ounces chocolate chips

Preheat the oven to 350 degrees. Fill twenty-four muffin cup liners (in muffin tins) about two-thirds full with the cake batter.

To make the filling, combine the cream cheese, egg, sugar, and salt in a mixer bowl and beat until creamy. Fold in the chocolate chips. Put a heaping tablespoonful of the filling into the center of each cupcake. Bake for 25-35 minutes or until a toothpick inserted in the center comes out clean. Do not overbake. No frosting required! Makes 24 cupcakes.

Sandy's Lemon Cake

This very moist lemon cake recipe is from Sandy Morrow, a good friend of my sister, Jan. It's famous for drawing a crowd to Wednesday night suppers at their church.

1 (1 pound, 2.25 ounce) box lemon cake mix

1 (3.4 ounce) package instant lemon pudding mix

4 eggs

3/4 cup oil

3/4 cup water

Glaze:

1 tablespoon water

2 tablespoons melted butter

1/3 cup lemon juice

2 cups powdered sugar

Preheat the oven to 350 degrees. Grease a 9 x 13-inch baking pan. Prepare the cake mix using the pudding mix, eggs, oil and water. Bake in the prepared pan for 35-45 minutes, until a toothpick inserted in the center comes out clean. While the cake is baking, prepare the glaze, mixing together all the ingredients until smooth. Pour the glaze over the warm cake and serve. Yields 10-12 servings.

Janets Welcome Bars

Janet Bartels is another wonderful friend and former co-worker. I miss Janet's sense of humor and always pleasant disposition.

First Layer:

1 (18.25-ounce) package yellow
    cake mix

1 egg

1/3 cup butter or margarine
    melted

Second Layer:

1 (14-ounce) can sweetened
    condensed milk

1/2 cup chopped pecans

1 egg

1 teaspoon vanilla

1/2 cup broken English toffee bits

Preheat the oven to 350 degrees. Grease a 15 x 10-inch jelly-roll pan. Combine the ingredients for the first layer and press this mixture into the bottom and up the sides of the prepared pan. Then combine the ingredients for the second layer and spread on top of first layer.

Bake for 20 minutes or until golden brown. Let cool and cut into bars.

Serves 12-15.

Vonda's Lemon Custard Cake

Thanks to Vonda Higbee, a treasured friend and Keeping Good Company staff member, for sharing this quick and easy recipe.

- 1 prepared angel food cake
- 1 (3.4 ounce) package instant lemon pudding mix
- 1½ cups cold milk
- 1 cup (8 ounces) sour cream
- 1 (21-ounce) can cherry or strawberry pie filling

Tear the angel food cake into bite-sized pieces. Place the pieces in a 9 x 13-inch pan. In a mixing bowl, combine the pudding mix, milk and sour cream. Beat until thickened, about 2 minutes. Spread over the cake pieces. Spoon the pie filling on top and chill until serving time.

Yields about 12 servings.

Heavenly Hash Cake

This is a sinfully rich cake, but I love to prepare it with young children who are learning the basics in the kitchen since it doesn't require a hot oven or sharp knives.

12 ounces chocolate chips

1 (8-ounce) container of Cool Whip or another whipped topping of your choice

1 cup pecans

1 small jar marshmallow cream ice cream topping

1 large prepared angel food cake, torn into pieces

Melt the chocolate chips in a heavy glass measuring cup in the microwave, stirring every minute for 2-3 minutes until smooth. Don't overcook. Stir the pecans into the chocolate. Fold in the whipped topping. Spray a large glass baking dish with vegetable oil and then arrange the angel food cake pieces over the bottom of the dish. Spread the chocolate mixture gently over the cake pieces and refrigerate for several hours or overnight before serving.

Serves 10~12.

Norma's Piecrust

Jana Agniel's mom, Norma Hughes, gets rave reviews for this piecrust. The word "crust" almost sounds too heavy for such a light treat! Thank you, Norma!

2 cups flour

1 cup shortening (Norma uses Crisco)

1/2 teaspoon salt

1 egg, beaten

1 tablespoon vinegar

3 tablespoons cold water

Preheat the oven to 400 degrees. Mix the flour, shortening, and salt with a pastry blender. Beat together the egg, vinegar and cold water. Add to the flour mixture, mixing well, but do not knead. Divide the dough in half. Roll on a floured surface until large enough to fit on a 9-inch pie plate. Carefully place the dough in the pie plate, crimping edges. Bake until golden brown, about 12-15 minutes, or use with any pie or quiche filling according to the directions.

Makes 2 crusts.

Paula's Coconut Cream Pie

Paula Shelden, another friend from my hometown church, shares this wonderful pie recipe with us.

3 cups milk

4 egg yolks

1 cup sugar

1/4 teaspoon salt

3 tablespoons cornstarch

1 teaspoon vanilla

3 tablespoons butter

1 cup shredded coconut

1 (9-inch) baked piecrust

Whipped cream for garnish

Heat 2 1/2 cups of the milk in a saucepan. Beat the egg yolks with the remaining 1/2 cup milk. Mix the sugar, salt and cornstarch. Add this mixture to the egg and milk mixture. Take 1/4 cup of the heated milk and add to the egg mixture. Then add this mixture to the rest of the heated milk. Cook over medium heat, stirring constantly, for about 10 minutes (until thick). Add the vanilla and butter and stir. Fold in the coconut. Pour into the baked piecrust. Let cool. When ready to serve, top with whipped cream. Serves 8.

Peanut Butter Chocolate CHEESECAKE BARS

Our family loves any dessert that resembles cheesecake. This has become one of my son's favorites. If you prefer, you may substitute milk chocolate chips for the semisweet chips.

crust:

2/3 cup brown sugar

2 cups flour

1 cup chopped pecans

2/3 cup butter, melted

Preheat the oven to 350 degrees. Mix the brown sugar, flour, pecans and melted butter until the mixture is crumbly. Press into the bottom of a 9 x 13-inch baking pan. Bake for 12-15 minutes or until light golden brown. Set aside while you prepare the filling.

Filling:

2 (8-ounce) packages cream cheese, softened

1 cup granulated sugar

¼ cup flour

½ cup milk

3 eggs

1 tablespoon vanilla

1 cup semisweet chocolate chips

3 tablespoons smooth peanut butter

Reduce the oven temperature to 325 degrees. Beat the cream cheese, granulated sugar, and flour in a large mixer bowl until smooth. Gradually beat in the milk, eggs, and vanilla. Microwave the chocolate chips in a medium-size glass measuring cup or bowl for 30 seconds at a time, stirring in between, until smooth and creamy. This should take a total of about 2 minutes of cooking time. Stir the peanut butter into the melted chocolate until well blended. Stir 1 cup of the cream cheese mixture into the chocolate mixture. Pour the remaining cream cheese mixture over crust. Pour the chocolate mixture over the cream cheese mixture and swirl the mixtures with a knife. Bake for 35-45 minutes, or until set. Cool completely in the pan on a wire rack. Refrigerate until firm. Cut into bars. Serves 12-15.

Donna's Chocolate Sauce

My dad's sweet wife, Donna Huisenga, contributed this versatile recipe. She prepared it in about 10 minutes one evening with ingredients that could be found even in the most basic of pantries. We have enjoyed it with ice cream cake and drizzled over brownies.

1 cup sugar

2 tablespoons cocoa

1 tablespoon butter

1/3 cup milk

1 teaspoon vanilla

Combine all the ingredients in a small saucepan and stir over medium heat until the mixture reaches a boil. Continue cooking for 2 minutes. Remove from the heat and put the pan into about 1 inch of cool water. Stir until the sauce thickens

Makes about 1 cup.

Raspberry Sauce

This simple sauce is delicious over ice cream, cheesecake, brownies ~ the list is endless!

1 (10 ounce) package frozen raspberries

½ cup sugar

1 tablespoon fresh lemon juice

Combine the raspberries, sugar, and lemon juice in a saucepan. Bring to a boil over low heat, stirring occasionally. Cook for 6-8 minutes. Press the sauce through a sieve into a bowl, discarding the seeds. Return the sauce to the saucepan. Cook over low heat until thickened, stirring constantly. Continue to cook until the mixture is reduced to about 3/4 cup. Chill immediately, stirring frequently while cooling. Any unused portion may be stored in an airtight container in the refrigerator for up to 2 weeks. Makes about 3/4 cup.

A Final Grace Note:

It is 6 AM and I am standing in our empty "old house". We left the children to sleep in at the "new house" so I could do a final cleaning here. In these moments of silence, I walk through each room taking it all in one last time. I discover that it's not the gentle curve of the driveway, or the velvety feel of the maple counter top in the kitchen, or even the breathtaking view out of the breakfast room window that makes me cry when I say good-bye to this place. It's only when I see the pencil marks on the doorjamb of the laundry room that became our family growth chart that I shed a few tears. This is where we have marked our progress over the past eight years. I remember how surprised and pleased we were to find how much taller each of the kids had grown in such a short amount of time. I think I understand now where the delight in this moment came from ~ we were growing not because of something we had done right, but possibly even in spite of what we had done wrong. That, my friends, is grace.

My prayer is that, no matter where life takes us, we will move through it, loving and learning and growing in grace.

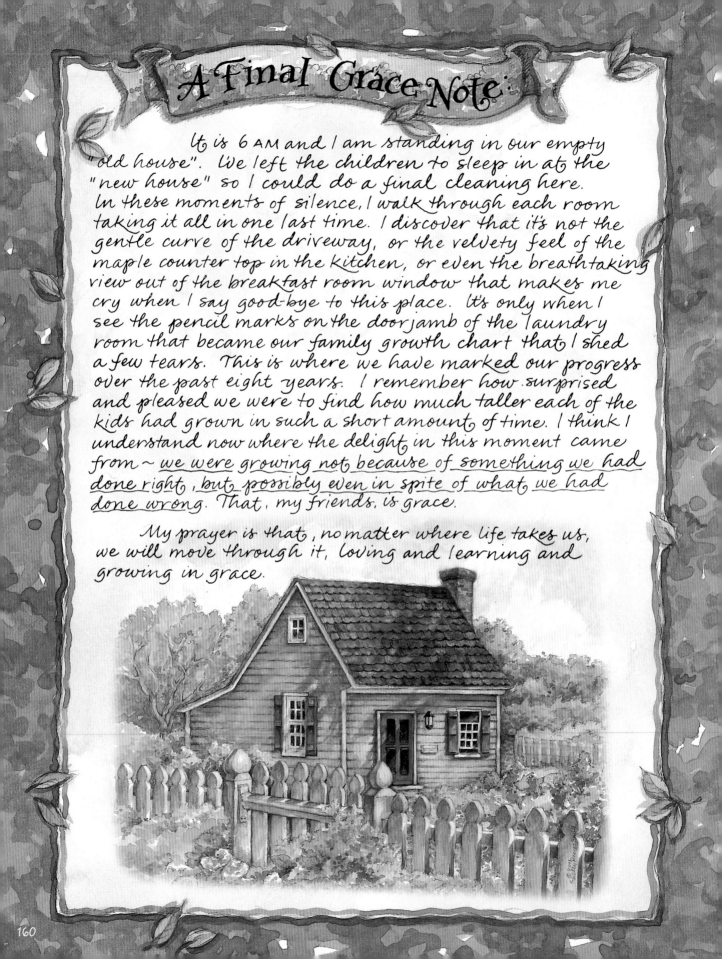

Index

C

cabbage
  green, in Thai Salad, 70
  red, in Pork Chops and Apples,
    106--107
Caesar Dip, 20
cake(s)
  Coffee, Buttery Streusel, 134-135
  Cupcakes, Cream Cheese, 148
  18-Karat Gold Neighbor, 146-147
  Heavenly Hash, 153
  Lemon, Sandy's, 149
  Lemon Custard, Vonda's, 152
  Pound, Cream Cheese, 132
  White Texas, 140-141
Camden County Catfish, 92-93
cantaloupe, in Such a Sassy Salsa, 16
Caramel Apple Dip, 9
carrots
  Company, 117
  in 18-Karat Gold Neighbor Cake,
    146-147
  in Sunday Morning Muffins, 38
casserole(s)
  Baja Lasagna, 94-95
  Broccoli au Gratin, 119
  Dino's Potatoes, 126
  Monterey Rice, 127
  Mushroom, 125
  My Mom's Sweet Potatoes, 114-115
  Sour Cream Noodle Bake, 101
  Spinach-Alfredo Lasagna, 85
  Vidalia Onion and Rice, 120
cheese(s)
  and Artichoke Torte, 12
  Asiago Mashed Potatoes, Garlic-, 118
  Biscuits, Country-Style, 27
  Brie, Baked, 6
  in Broccoli au Gratin, 119
  in Brooke's Tex-Mex Chicken
    Dinner, 82-83
  Chicken, Soup, 52
  in Fiesta Quiche, 97
  Mozzarella, Zucchini with, 122
  in Quesadillas, 8
  in Tomato Tart, 102-103

cheesecake
  Bars, Peanut Butter Chocolate,
    156-157
  Blueberry-Lemon, Dee's, 136-138
  Tarts, Pumpkin, 133
Cherry Dessert, Margie's, 142-143
chicken
  Amandine, 90-91
  in Baja Lasagna, 94-95
  in Brooke's Tex-Mex Dinner, 82

  Cheese Soup, 52
  Fingers with Honey Mustard, 14-15
  in Lettuce Wraps, 10-11
  Pot Pie, 88-89
  Salad, Oriental, 72-73
  in Oodles of Noodles, 60-61
  in Southwest Sunburst Salad, 68-69
chocolate
  Cheesecake Bars, Peanut Butter,
    156-157
  Chip Cheese Bars, Myra's Rich, 139
  Chocolate Chip Muffins, 44-45
  Sauce, Donna's, 158
Chowder, Corn, 58
Citrus Vinaigrette, 78
Coconut Cream Pie, Paula's, 155
Coffee Cake, Buttery Streusel, 134-135
Coleslaw, Shirley's Crunchy, 63
Company Carrots, 117
Connor's Lemon-Blueberry Muffins,
  40-41

cookies
  Janet's Welcome Bars, 150-151
  Myra's Rich Chocolate Chip
    Cheese Bars, 139
  Peanut Butter Chocolate
    Cheesecake Bars, 156-157
  Peanut Butter Cup, 144-145
corn
  Bread Croutons, 77
  Bread Salad, Missouri, 64-65

Chowder, 58
Muffins, Sweet, 42-43
in Southwest Sunburst Salad, 68-69
Country-Style Cheese Biscuits, 27
cream cheese
  Cupcakes, 148
  Frosting, 147
  Pound Cake, 132
  Spread, 48
Cream of Tomato Soup, 59
Croutons, Corn Bread, 77

D

Dee's Blueberry-Lemon Cheesecake,
  136-138
desserts. *See also* cake(s); chocolate;
  cookies; pie(s); tarts
  Margie's Cherry Dessert, 142-143
  Pound Cake Muffins, 39
Dino's Potatoes, 126

162

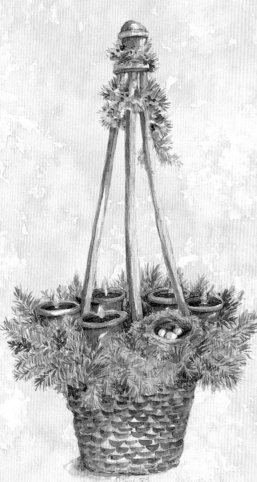